chocolate bar

chocolate bar

recipes and entertaining ideas for living the sweet life

alison nelson and matt lewis

Photographs by Brian Kennedy
Recipes by Lillian Chou, Matt Lewis, and Alison Nelson

A Stonesong Press Book

Printed in China

Produced by Stonesong Press, LLC
27 West 24th Street, Suite 510
New York, NY 10010

Chocolate Bar, LLC
48 Eighth Avenue
New York, NY 10014

Library of Congress Control Number 2004090702
ISBN 0-7624-1921-0

A Stonesong Press Book
Edited by Jennifer Kasius
Book design by Alicia Freile
Typography: Arial, Blur, and Interstate
First Edition
10 9 8 7 6 5 4 3 2 1

This book may be ordered by mail from the publisher. Please include $2.50 for postage and handling.
But try your bookstore first!

Running Press Book Publishers
125 South Twenty-second Street
Philadelphia, PA 19103-4399

Visit us on the web!
www.runningpress.com

Recipe Credits:
Recipe on pages 46—48 used with permission of Lesli Heffler
Recipe for Chocolate Fudge Layer Cake on page 50 is reprinted from Diner Desserts©by Tish Boyle and used with permission of Chronicle Books LLC, San Francisco.
Recipes on pages 53—54 used with permission of Tammy Ogletree of CookieChick
Recipe for Chocolate Ganache Icing on page 54 used with permission of Lesli Heffler
Recipe on page 76 used with permission of Nick Malgieri
Recipes on page 92 used with permission of Andrew Shotts of Garrison Confections
Recipe on page 96 used with permission of by Chef Ilene C. Shane of SweetBliss
Recipe on page 164 used with permission of Nancy Mongiovi
Recipe on page 166 used with permission of Jacques Torres of MrChocolate.com LLC

Photo Credits
Pages 16—17: Photo taken at Miss America Diner, Jersey City, N.J.
Page 65: Reproduced with permission of Culver Pictures.
Pages 100—101: Photo taken at The Courtyard of The New York Palace Hotel
Page 108—110: Photos taken at Keens Steakhouse, New York City
Pages 145—151: Photos taken at Garrison Confections, Providence, R.I.

For our moms,

Gail Lewis and Megan McGonigal,

for passing on their love of all things chocolate

CONTENTS

ACKNOWLEDGMENTS

We thought opening a store in Manhattan was difficult until we faced the task of writing and developing this book. The process of cobbling together the text, the photos, and the recipes was made infinitely easier and ten times more enjoyable because of the time, energy, and devotion of the many friends and cohorts involved. We, the harried and humble authors, wish to give special thanks (in no particular order) to each and every person that spent time in our chocolate world:

Brian Kennedy for each and every photograph and everything in between

Lillian Chou for matching the recipes to our very specific and skewed vision

Alison Fargis of The Stonesong Press for seeking us out and guiding us through

Lesli Heffler for the labors of recipe testing, food styling, and answering our desperate calls

Brittany Williams for testing and tasting

Laura Tucker for anticipating and creating our every design need

Ilene C. Shane of SweetBliss for your gooey influence and the black and white

Andrew C. Shotts of Garrison Confections for the midnight pie fix and the salted caramel

Jacques Torres of Jacques Torres Chocolates for the kind advice and the hottest hot chocolate

Nick Malgieri for the good counsel and the dog-eared copy of his masterpiece, *Chocolate*

Ken, Kris, and Lissa at Jacques Torres Chocolate, for keeping us on our toes

Tammy Ogletree of CookieChick for keeping the cookies ridiculously addictive

Janet Olguin a.k.a. Suki for keeping us together at the seams

Megan McGonigal for recipe testing and babysitting

Gail "Ma" Lewis for introducing the "Chocolate as Breakfast" philosophy

Myra Fiori and Sarah Lyon at illy for all our coffee needs

Matt Holbein a.k.a. Bandit for doing the truckin' thang

Adam Nelson, Ryan Urcia, and all at Workhouse Publicity for making sure we always show off our best side

Nancy Mongiovi and the "kids" for exfoliating with us

Lulu Scout Nelson for not holding this book against her mother.

Larry, the carpenter, for rescuing us from our sometimes not so handy selves

Miles Seaton, Thea Karwoski, Katie Jewitt, Anna Van Meter, Carolyn Murnyck, Ed Baer, William Meny, and the rest of the CB crew for the outstanding lattes, pretty chalk boards, crafty displays and wonderful diversions.

Models Inc.: MJ Trussell, Janet Olguin, Daniel Bellury, Kevin Schaeffer, Carolyn Murnick, Ryan Vanderhoof, Edward Baer, Tara Coppola, Carmella Crimeni, Dylan Roadie, Renee Loger

Downtown &
Brooklyn
via 8 Av Express
A
To Lefferts Blvd or Far Rockaway.
PM rush hours also to Rockaway Park
Late nights on local track

OUR PHILOSOPHY

relax. enjoy. have fun. eat more chocolate.

expect variety. classic treats.

retro reconfigured. nouveau flavor

combos. experiment. update.

change shape. change colors.

change your mind. change of heart.

never fussy. never stuffy.

always fresh. nothing preserved.

nothing reserved. au natural.

eat a lot more chocolate.

INTRODUCTION

the very brief background

We first conceived of the idea for our store, Chocolate Bar, over a chocolate layer cake on a snowy Saturday evening at Matt's house. In true Chocolate Bar style, Matt had made the cake and Alison ate it. Over the next four months we consumed lots of chocolate while renovating an old packing and shipping store in New York's West Village. We each took turns pulling up archaic tile, painting walls, sanding things that needed to be sanded, and fine-tuning design that, well, needed fine-tuning. The idea was to turn this tiny storefront into a spectacular showcase for high-quality chocolates made right here in New York City by some superb chefs. We purposely steered clear from the preciousness that surrounds so much quality chocolate—no gold, no lace, no frilly froufrou. It was (and is) all about selling chocolate without intimidation. Chocolate is fun!

we open

Opening day was both a delight and a horror. We knew people loved chocolate but we certainly underestimated how much. The crowds were large and hungry. The paint was still wet, and the chocolates were still being produced when we opened our doors. Like any new business, we were a bit lost ("What is this button on the register for?" "How do I order more milk?") but managed to get through the first day with a more than enthusiastic response from those willing to wait in line. To our surprise, we were utterly taken aback by the general consumer's interest in all things chocolate. Questions went beyond the typical, "What's in the salted caramel truffle?" to "What brand of chocolate and what percentage of cacao is used to make the salted caramel?" It was extraordinary. Our customers were becoming chocolate all-stars. Don't get us wrong; they could still enjoy a brownie and a steaming cup of hot chocolate, but they were genuinely interested in the finer points of chocolate and, more importantly, they were having a great time.

a few months later

Still bleary-eyed (opening a new store is an experience best experienced when you don't require a lot of sleep) and living on a strict diet of cookies, chocolate, and caffeine, we took our philosophy directly to the people by giving "chocolate tastings" to various groups. These tastings were mostly laid-back affairs with attentive chocolate addicts sipping wine and sparkling water between numerous mouthfuls of truffles and chocolate bars. We relayed chocolate's history, the medical and scientific facts, dispelled myths, defined chocolate terms, and ate a lot of chocolate. We were (and are) having a great time spreading the chocolate gospel. We were (and still are) in desperate need of greens and fiber.

now

The store is still moving and grooving and we still give tastings on a regular basis. This book is our opportunity to share the "chocolate lifestyle" with you. We hope you enjoy it. We hope you incorporate the recipes into your revolving repertoire. And finally, we hope you write to your government officials and urge them to make chocolate and caffeine a respectable and highly prescribed part of a well-balanced diet. And yes, even now, we're still eating a lot of chocolate.

—matt and alison

classic chocolate redefined

We love the classics.

There is something satisfying about the simplicity and purity of a chocolate-chip cookie. There is endless joy in a standard and honest brownie. Nothing could be sexier than a slab of diner chocolate layer cake accompanied by a glass of whole milk.

Over the years, the classic chocolate desserts have been tweaked, abused, reduced, and disguised. We love some of these new twists (lime brownies) and hate a lot of them (yam-papaya-chocolate-chip cookies, no-fat chocolate cake). Our goal in this chapter is to take you back to the roots of these classics with just a few minor variations. We treat the classics with great respect—subtracting a bit of sugar here, adding some dark chocolate there—but otherwise we remain true to the ideal.

Our aim is to redefine the classics, not reinvent them.

KEEP IT SIMPLE

We like to keep baking simple: simple ingredients, simple instructions, simple clean up. Simply put: If you aren't having fun while making it, it probably won't be any fun to eat.

Avoid the seduction of "recipe porn," which will tempt you with a litany of exotic ingredients and gorgeous, glossy, perfect (and often impossible to replicate in real life) photos. Just reading about chocolate curls, essence of extract, and unusual and useless tools will make you salivate and sweat. Resistance is hard but not futile. If it makes you feel better, we too are often seduced by these extraordinary feats in pastry arts. But like you, we have jobs and family and friends and appointments, and we don't have the time or stamina to re-create these works of art. Let's leave the

sublime artistry to the extremely talented and well-trained pastry chefs. If a recipe calls for more than four pots, pans, or bowls, chances are we've never made it and never will.

However simple and pure our Chocolate Bar recipes are, the same cannot be said of our lives. We would like to tell you that our home kitchens are master-planned models of efficiency. We want to tell you that items are labeled, recipes are filed, and dishes and cups are matched and stacked neatly in their correct places. We wish we could tell you that we buy only the necessary kitchen tools, gadgets, and baking supplies and never buy any ridiculous kitchen gizmos from late-night infomercials. We want to tell you that we never purchase magazines and cookbooks full of recipes that we never intend to re-create. Yes, we wish we could tell you these things, but that would be a hideous stretch of the truth, if not an outright lie.

Our lives are complicated; our recipes are simple.

FIZZLE THE DRIZZLE

A rather strange and unexplained phenomenon has taken firm root in the chocolate world. We refer to this trend as the Chocolate Drizzle Debacle. As far as we can tell, this tragedy began in five-star kitchens, bubbled over slowly to the casual dining chains, and now permeates every corner of the universe, including mom-and-pop shops, home dining rooms, and gasp . . . there have even been reports of seeing the dreaded chocolate drizzle in school cafeterias.

You're familiar with this phenomenon. Warm chocolate tarts and vanilla bean ice cream are often the main targets of the drizzle. The chocolate is interwoven and crisscrossed on the plate in an artistic, often weblike, arrangement. Lately, pies, brownies, and even cookies have been victims of the drizzle.

Chocolate drizzle has a lot going for it: It's simple to make and squirt; it's pretty; it's showy. What many people don't realize about this resourceful enemy of the chocolate world, however, is its many weaknesses: It's often redundant, overused, and boring.

Would you be happy with a "drizzle" of ice cream on your hot apple pie? How about a "drizzle" of whipped cream on your pumpkin pie? Think of Thanksgiving with just a "drizzle" of gravy on your mashed potatoes.

Don't get too precious with desserts; we want them soaking. Pick up an ice cream scoop and load heaps of vanilla ice cream onto your brownie, then drown it in fudge sauce—c'mon, let's see that brownie swim! It's okay, really—don't be afraid. Melt slabs of chocolate and douse that chocolate torte.

Go overboard: That is the point of dessert, after all.

PRESENTATION IS, WELL, ALMOST EVERYTHING

> *"The setting must be viewed as a whole. Harmonious plate or platter arrangements can be ruined if they clash with the table color scheme or the lighting of the room."—Mary Albert Wenker,* The Art of Serving Food Attractively, 1951

Chocolate is inherently giddy. You don't really need to dress it up to serve it because people tend to want/desire/crave chocolate in any form. The same, alas, cannot be said of beets, cauliflower, or cabbage, and that's why we won't speak of them ever again.

Chocolate adapts well to any presentation, so feel free to experiment—there are no constraints. We have provided you with a few pointers to get started:

Bigger Is Better

■ Refuse to cut "small" cake, brownie, or pie slices. What is the point?

■ Give people large forks and big spoons (soup spoons work well) to eat their desserts with—traditional dessert utensils are too often petite, uninspired, and excruciatingly quaint.

■ Put big chocolate desserts in tiny bowls. Why? Because it makes the dessert look more fun and abundant. We're not sure why this works, but it does. Stop asking questions.

■ Increase the cookie girth. Don't be afraid of the 8-inch-diameter chocolate-chip monster.

Beyond the Paper Plates

Stark-white porcelain provides a great backdrop for chocolate desserts, but you don't have to be an extreme minimalist. Feel free to introduce some color on your plates and serving bowls—blues and oranges complement chocolate well.

Find another use for that never-used punch bowl. It's perfect for pudding, bonbons, cookies, and iced chocolate.

Ignore the servingware standards: Put truffles in soufflé dishes, stack cookies in mugs, chill your gelatin in a sundae glass. Mix it up.

Feel free to break out Grandma's china to serve that great ice cream sundae. Dust off your crystal to serve a simple malted.

Eye Candy

Powdered sugar is messy. Use it more often on brownies, chocolate cakes, and cookies.

Who said candles are for birthdays and special occasions? Put candles in all chocolate desserts for almost any reason. Did a check bounce? Coping with a major breakup? Put a candle in something chocolaty, and make someone or yourself feel special for no particular reason.

Stop stacking brownies. Lay them out flat to spell friends' names, odd words, and favorite quotes. (The dot above the "i" is usually served well with a big round cookie.)

Variety is important and visually appealing. Mix up dark, milk, and white chocolate confections.

Label everything. Some people might want to be warned about your latest chocolate experiment, and more importantly, people might have allergies to liquor, coffee, or certain infused essences. Use simple typed index cards for descriptions or jazz it up with a heavy cardstock.

■ Use the ribbon and wrap! Even a single cupcake seems special when presented in a simple box tied with satin ribbon.

■ Bigger is better but clutter can be deadly. Remember, if you're hosting a dinner party or a chocolate tasting, you should steer clear of clutter. Leave the gold lamé napkins and ruffled lace in the closet. The plates, serving ware, and linens should add to, not subtract from, the food's taste. Let the food be the center of attention.

HOLIDAYS WITH A TWIST

Every holiday should be a chocolate holiday. Here are our thoughts, suggestions, and rants on how to increase your chocolate intake each month of the year:

New Year's Eve

Use the cheap champagne you received last year to make champagne truffles—they are perfect for large parties and drunken guests. Simply replace the Armagnac with champagne in our Chocolate Truffle recipe (page 40) and follow the regular directions.

Valentine's Day

Make it a dark and spicy evening. Dark chocolate with a hint of smoky ground chipotle chilies makes for an unusual and warm dessert, whether they are combined in a cup of cocoa or a special baked treat.

St. Patrick's Day

Forget about the green beer. Serve chocolate beer instead. Now available from several American and European breweries, you can find different kinds at your local liquor store or beverage center. To get those mouths and eyes smiling, serve handmade dark chocolate truffles with pints of stout.

Easter

Liven up your chocolate eggs with a cocoa-butter paint job. Follow the basic techniques on page 163 to create your masterpiece.

Mother's Day

There is nothing like a box of chocolates to make Mom happy, but if you want something different, try making her breakfast in bed and serve her banana chocolate-chip pancakes (page 56) alongside a steaming cup of joe. Your mom deserves the best so, please, use the highest-quality chocolate you can find.

Father's Day

Dad does not need another tie or golf knickknack. Make him a batch of chocolate-chip cookies or some sort of variation (page 53). If you insist on buying him a tie, use it to tie up a box of homemade truffles.

Fourth of July

Today is America's birthday, so make the old girl a chocolate birthday cake—complete with speckled white frosting (page 35) and red, white, and blue sprinkles. To finish off, add sparklers!

Halloween

This is a chocolate-lover's holiday! If you need more of the sweet stuff, try toasted pumpkin seeds covered in dark chocolate. (To make: Preheat oven to 250° F. Cover a sheet pan with parchment paper and evenly spread out at least 1 cup of fresh seeds from your just-carved jack-o-lantern. Sprinkle lightly with salt. Toast seeds in oven for 10 minutes or until seeds look lightly golden. Let seeds cool to room temperature. Transfer seeds to a bowl and cover pan with a new sheet of parchment paper. Melt 8 ounces of good quality bittersweet chocolate (double boiler or microwave method) until smooth. Remove from heat and stir in ⅔ cup of toasted pumpkin seeds. Spread mixture onto parchment paper and sprinkle with remaining ⅓ cup of pumpkin seeds. Press the seeds lightly into the mixture. Chill for approximately 1 hour. Break into pieces and serve.)

Thanksgiving

Chocolate Pumpkin Pie tastes great and makes sense. Simply apply a thin layer of melted chocolate to the inside of your crust to protect your crisp, golden pie from becoming a soggy and sullen mess. Just wait for the melted chocolate layer to cool before adding the pumpkin filling.

Hanukah

Three words: Chocolate Dipped Matzoh. To make: Prep your chocolate for dipping by melting 8 ounces of chocolate, stir in 2 tablespoons of unsalted butter until melted and the mixture is shiny, dip your matzoh in the chocolate, and place on waxed paper to cool.

Christmas

This is the perfect time of the year for chocolate overload. Here are just a few of a thousand pointers:

- All hot chocolate must be stirred with a candy cane.

- Don't you think Santa might be a little tired of cookies and milk? Surprise the fat man with a slice of chocolate soufflé tart (page 96) and an egg cream (page 90).

- Get molding! Forget about the traditional Christmas ornaments and mold some chocolate ones as gifts. Don't be afraid to paint with cocoa butter, dazzle with edible gold and silver flakes, or coat with colored sanding sugar.

- Wish them a sweet holiday with a custom-wrapped chocolate bar. Get creative on your computer or use construction paper and crayons. It's a gift and card in one!

classic recipes

johnnie walker black chocolate pudding

YIELD: SIX 8-OUNCE CUPS

Deep, dark, and fortified with a good smooth whiskey, this pudding is perfect for outdoor parties, nightcaps, and after-dinner decadence. The alcohol works perfectly with the chocolate—not too overpowering—but feel free to omit it completely or substitute a different liquor such as Grand Marnier or Cognac. Top with fresh whipped cream (see sidebar) and sprinkle with cocoa.

3½ ounces bittersweet chocolate, chopped into small pieces
2 cups milk
½ cup heavy cream
¾ cup sugar
2 tablespoons cornstarch
3 large egg yolks
1 teaspoon vanilla extract
3 tablespoons Johnnie Walker Black Scotch whiskey
2 tablespoons cocoa powder to taste

Place the chocolate in a large mixing bowl. Bring the milk, cream, and ¼ cup of the sugar to a boil in a heavy 2-quart saucepan.

Sift the cornstarch into a small bowl and whisk in the remaining ½ cup of sugar.

Whisk the egg yolks in a medium bowl and add the cornstarch mixture. Add the vanilla and whisk until combined well.

When the milk mixture comes to a boil, pour one-third of it into the egg mixture, whisking constantly. Add another third and whisk again. Return the egg-and-milk mixture to the pan. Reduce the heat to moderate and whisk constantly until the mixture begins to boil and thicken. Continue to whisk the boiling mixture for 3 minutes.

Remove from the heat, pour through a strainer directly over the chocolate, and whisk gently until the chocolate is melted and incorporated. Add the whiskey and whisk until smooth. Let the mixture cool for about 10 minutes. Cover the mixture with plastic wrap, making sure that the pudding surface comes in direct contact with the plastic wrap.

Alternately, pour the pudding into individual cups, ramekins, or martini glasses and cover separately. Sprinkle with cocoa powder, to taste.

Refrigerate for 6 hours or overnight, until the mixture is chilled thoroughly and very thick.

it's basic: whip your cream

We admit it; some things are too laborious to be considered worthwhile. You will not catch us scraping out pumpkins to make pumpkin pie it s a fantastic idea but the reality is quite terrifying. We are, however, converts to the make-your-own-fresh-whipped-cream school (and we put it on everything). It s easy, delicious, and soul satisfying.

Toss the can, follow these instructions:

Yield: 2 cups

2 cups heavy cream
¼ cup granulated or confectioners sugar
1 to 2 teaspoons extract (orange, mint, or almond) to taste (optional)

The obsessive-compulsive whip creamers recommend two things:
1) use a metal mixing bowl ONLY
2) you must chill your equipment (mixing bowl, beaters/whisks) in the freezer 15 minutes prior to beginning

Whip the cream at medium-high speed in a metal mixing bowl. Once it reaches that blissful, billowy state and before the soft peaks form, slowly add the sugar and extract while beating. Continue until the soft peaks form and your cream has almost doubled in volume. Use immediately on pies, tarts, cakes, ice cream, hot chocolate or just eat from the bowl!

red velvet cake

YIELD: 1 TRIPLE-LAYER 8-INCH CAKE

We love Red Velvet Cake! It is towering, loud, brash, slightly trashy, and perfect for any party. This cake almost always shows up at our holiday parties in November and December, and it makes its requisite appearance on Valentine's Day, but you can bake it for any occasion.

The crumb on this cake is slightly flaky and fluffy, which lends itself perfectly to the rich vanilla icing.

4 tablespoons good-quality cocoa powder such as Valrhona
1 ounce red food coloring (1 bottle; see Note)
2½ cups cake flour
1 teaspoon salt
1 cup buttermilk
1 teaspoon vanilla extract
6 tablespoons (¾ stick) unsalted butter
1½ tablespoons shortening at room temperature
1⅔ cups sugar
2 eggs
1 egg yolk
2 tablespoons boiling water
1 tablespoon white vinegar
1 teaspoon baking soda

Preheat the oven to 350° F and place a rack in the middle position. Butter and flour the sides of three 8-inch round cake tins and line the bottoms with parchment circles (butter the parchment as well).

In a small bowl, whisk together the cocoa powder, red food coloring, and 2 tablespoons of boiling water. Set aside to cool.

Sift the flour and salt together. In a separate bowl, mix the buttermilk and vanilla together.

In a standing mixer fitted with the paddle attachment, cream the butter and shortening on high speed until light and fluffy. Add the sugar and continue beating for approximately 5 minutes until pale and fluffy.

Add the eggs and yolk one at a time, blending well after each addition.

Alternately add the flour mixture and buttermilk, beginning and ending with flour. Mix until combined.

Dissolve the baking soda in the vinegar (the mixture will fizz) and add to the mixer until just combined.

Divide the batter evenly into the prepared pans, smoothing the tops and tapping gently on the bottoms and sides to remove any air bubbles. Bake for 30 minutes, or until a tester inserted comes out with a few moist crumbs.

Cool on a rack for 10 minutes; invert tins to release the cakes. Cool to room temperature, and make the frosting while the cakes are cooling. Use a serrated knife to level off the tops of the cakes until they are perfectly flat and even.

Note: Red food coloring adds a gorgeous tint to this cake but may stain plastics as well as your clothes, so be careful when using it.

speckled white frosting

Vanilla beans give a wonderful look and flavor to this white frosting. But if a pure, "non-speckled" frosting is preferred, simply replace the vanilla paste with 1 teaspoon of vanilla extract.

1½ cups sugar
6 tablespoons all-purpose flour
1½ cups milk
6 tablespoons heavy cream
3 sticks unsalted butter, softened and cut into 1-inch cubes
2¼ teaspoons vanilla paste

In a 1-quart heavy saucepan, whisk together the sugar and flour. Add the milk and cream and bring to a boil over high heat, whisking constantly. Reduce to medium heat and stir constantly for 3 minutes. Transfer the mixture to a standing mixer fitted with the paddle attachment. Mix on high speed until cool. Reduce the speed to low and add the butter, until incorporated. Add the vanilla paste and mix until combined.

Allow the frosting to chill for about 1 hour before using. If too soft, it can cause the cake layers to slide. If it becomes too hard, it can be softened over a pot of simmering water

Using an offset spatula, spread a thin layer of buttercream on each cake layer and smooth out the top before placing another cake layer on top. Finish the surface of the cake with a slightly thicker layer and even out the sides.

Decorate as you wish. For a beautiful, simple garnish, reserve some crumbs from the cake (easily rubbed off the sides before frosting) and sprinkle minimally on top. Chill for 1 hour before serving. Keep refrigerated, loosely covered with plastic wrap. (Frosting absorbs refrigerator odors easily.)

Note: This recipe makes a generous amount of frosting. Feel free to set some aside for an indulgent midnight snack.

truffles galore

There is nothing more enticing than a chocolate truffle, and these are classic renditions. Alcohol is optional of course, but the rolling technique remains the same for all three. Quantities are generous in each batch to encourage giving and sharing.

The amount of chocolate specified for coating is more than you will need but allows you to have enough to coat your truffles easily. Simply reserve any leftover chocolate for another use.

Truffles Grand Marnier

YIELD: ABOUT 4 DOZEN

This is the classic of classics. While using Grand Marnier is optional, these truffles are extra special because they are coated with chocolate first, both for easier handling and an extra dimension in eating.

Ganache:

12 ounces bittersweet chocolate, chopped into small pieces
1 cup heavy cream
¼ cup Grand Marnier
2 tablespoons unsalted butter, at room temperature

Coating:

12 ounces bittersweet chocolate, melted and tempered (page 160)
About ¼ cup confectioners' sugar or good-quality cocoa powder

Prepare the ganache:

Place the chocolate in a large mixing bowl; in a saucepan, bring the heavy cream just to a boil. Remove from the heat, pour over the chocolate, and gently whisk until smooth. Let sit for 3 minutes and add the Grand Marnier. Whisk gently until smooth. Scrape down the sides of the bowl; add the butter, then mix again. Cover with plastic wrap, making sure the

surface comes in direct contact with the plastic wrap. Let sit in a cool room or refrigerate for 6 hours, or until firm.

Roll the truffles:

Scoop rounded teaspoons of the mixture onto a baking sheet lined with parchment or waxed paper. Truffles should not be perfectly round, so don't worry if the balls are somewhat misshapen. Roll them between your hands to shape slightly and freeze for 30 minutes while you temper the chocolate.

Line a large baking sheet with parchment paper and place a mound of cocoa powder or confectioners' sugar at one end of the sheet.

Temper the chocolate as directed on page 160. Dip your fingers in the chocolate, then roll each truffle back and forth in your fingertips, coating the truffle with chocolate (be sure the coating is thick enough). Be careful, as your palms tend to be warmer and can untemper the chocolate. Dip your hands in chocolate as necessary and occasionally wipe your hands against the side of the bowl of chocolate to remove excess. Stir the chocolate occasionally to keep it tempered. Just before the chocolate sets, drop the chocolate-coated truffles into cocoa powder or confectioners' sugar, rolling gently with a fork to coat. Repeat and gently roll the dusted truffles toward the back end of the tray. The chocolate will set as you progress. You may see some filling peeking out of an uncoated area as the chocolate begins to set. Simply dab the area lightly with a finger full of chocolate to seal.

Store the truffles in layers in small fluted candy cups or between sheets of parchment or waxed paper in airtight containers, refrigerated, for up to 2 weeks and frozen up to 3 months. Let sit, covered, at room temperature for 30 minutes before serving.

Espresso Truffles

YIELD: ABOUT 3 DOZEN

Coffee and chocolate are such a classic combination. This version uses instant espresso, which concentrates flavor while avoiding any further addition of liquid, making a dense, rich treat.

Ganache:

10 ounces milk chocolate, chopped into small pieces
1 cup heavy cream
1 tablespoon instant espresso granules
1 tablespoon unsalted butter, at room temperature

Coating:

12 ounces milk chocolate, melted and tempered (see page 160)

Prepare the ganache:

Place the chocolate in a large mixing bowl; in a saucepan, bring the heavy cream just to a boil. Remove from the heat immediately and pour over the chocolate, whisking gently until smooth. Let sit for 3 minutes and add the espresso granules. Whisk gently until smooth and thoroughly combined. Add the butter and scrape down the sides of the bowl, then mix again. Cover with plastic wrap, making sure the surface comes in direct contact with the plastic, and let sit in a cool room or refrigerate for 6 hours, or until firm.

Roll the truffles:

Scoop rounded teaspoons of the mixture onto a baking sheet lined with parchment or waxed paper. Truffles should not be perfectly round, so don't worry if the balls are somewhat misshapen. Smooth out any sharp edges and freeze for 30 minutes while you temper the chocolate.

Line a large baking sheet with parchment and place a mound of coarse or sanding sugar at one end of the sheet.

Temper the chocolate as directed on page 160. Dip your fingers in chocolate, then roll each truffle back and forth in your fingertips, coating the truffle with chocolate (be sure the coating is thick enough). Be careful, as your palms tend to be warmer and can untemper the chocolate. Dip your hands in the chocolate as necessary and occasionally wipe your hands against the sides of the bowl of chocolate to remove excess. Stir the chocolate occasionally to keep it tempered. Place the chocolate-coated truffles on parchment. The chocolate will set as you progress. You may see some filling peeking out of an uncoated area as the chocolate begins to set. Simply dab the area lightly with a finger full of chocolate to seal. When the chocolate begins to set, coat once more in the tempered chocolate for a thick coating to make the truffle less fragile.

Store the truffles in layers in small fluted candy cups or between sheets of parchment or waxed paper in airtight containers, refrigerated, for up to 2 weeks and frozen up to 3 months. Let sit covered at room temperature for 30 minutes before serving.

Pearls of Perigord (Truffles Armagnac)

YIELD: ABOUT 3 DOZEN

Armagnac comes from the Perigord region of southwest France. This classic combination gets its name from the shape and look of the sugar crystals that coat the velvety white interior of this confection. Because the filling is silky and unctuous, these truffles are a bit tricky to roll. Freezing helps them stay firm, but make sure they are completely coated in chocolate.

Ganache:

9 ounces white chocolate, chopped into very small pieces

2 tablespoons (1½ ounces) almond paste, softened (see Note)

½ cup heavy cream

2 tablespoons Armagnac

Coating:

12 ounces bittersweet chocolate, melted and tempered (see page 160)

⅔ cup coarse or sanding sugar (available from specialty shops)

Prepare the ganache:

Place the chocolate in a large mixing bowl and set aside. Place the softened almond paste in a large bowl. In a saucepan, heat the heavy cream just to a boil. Slowly add half the heavy cream to the almond paste, whisking constantly until smooth. Add the remaining cream and whisk until smooth. (The almond paste may be very hard and crumbly. If it's difficult to smooth, use a firm rubber spatula or wooden spoon and force against a mesh strainer with some cream until smooth.) Return to the saucepan and heat until just boiling; pour over the white chocolate and gently whisk until smooth. Let sit for 3 minutes and add the Armagnac. Whisk gently until well combined. Scrape down the sides of the bowl and mix again. Cover with plastic wrap, making sure the surface comes directly in contact with the plastic and refrigerate for 6 hours, or until firm.

Roll the truffles:

Scoop rounded teaspoons of the mixture onto a baking sheet lined with parchment or waxed paper. Truffles should not be perfectly round, so don't worry if the balls are somewhat misshapen. Smooth out any sharp edges and freeze for 30 minutes while you temper the chocolate. (This mixture is softer than the others, so work quickly when coating. If you find the filling becomes too soft, return it to the freezer until it's firm enough to work with.)

Line a large baking sheet with parchment and place a mound of coarse or sanding sugar at one end.

Temper the chocolate as directed on page 160. Dip your fingers in chocolate, then roll each truffle back and forth in your fingertips, coating the truffle with chocolate (be sure the coating is thick enough). Be careful, as your palms tend to be warmer and can untemper the chocolate. Dip your hands in chocolate as necessary and occasionally wipe your hands against the side of the bowl of chocolate to remove excess. Stir the chocolate occasionally to keep it tempered. Before they set, gently drop the chocolate-coated truffles into coarse or sanding sugar, rolling them gently with a fork to coat. Repeat and gently roll the sugared truffles towards the back end of the tray. The chocolate will set as you progress. You may see some filling peeking out of an uncoated area as the chocolate begins to set. Simply dab the area lightly with a finger full of chocolate to seal.

Store the truffles in layers in small fluted candy cups or between sheets of parchment or waxed paper in airtight containers, refrigerated, for up to 2 weeks and frozen up to 3 months. Let sit, covered, at room temperature for 30 minutes before serving.

Note: If the almond paste is hard or seems crystallized, microwave it on low heat for 10 to 15 seconds at a time until soft to the touch. Keep the almond paste tightly sealed in plastic wrap.

dark chocolate ice cream with white chocolate swirl

YIELD: 1 QUART

Homemade ice cream is fun to make and tastes far better than the commercial varieties. This recipe creates a creamy, deep-chocolate ice cream accompanied by a sweet swirl of white chocolate. Feel free to add any variety of extras, such as crushed cookies, M&M's, and chunks of solid chocolate.

You will need an ice cream maker to make this recipe, which may seem cumbersome at first, but you'll find it well worth the effort when you taste the results.

White Chocolate Swirl:

½ cup white chocolate chips

½ cup heavy cream

Rich Chocolate Ice Cream:

1 cup heavy cream

2 cups milk

½ cup sugar

¼ teaspoon salt

5 large egg yolks

2 tablespoon light corn syrup

½ cup bittersweet chocolate (60 to 72% cacao), melted

Place the white chocolate chips in a heatproof bowl. Bring the ½ cup of cream to a boil in a heavy 1-quart saucepan and pour it over the chocolate. Gently whisk until smooth and chill, covered, in the refrigerator for 2 hours.

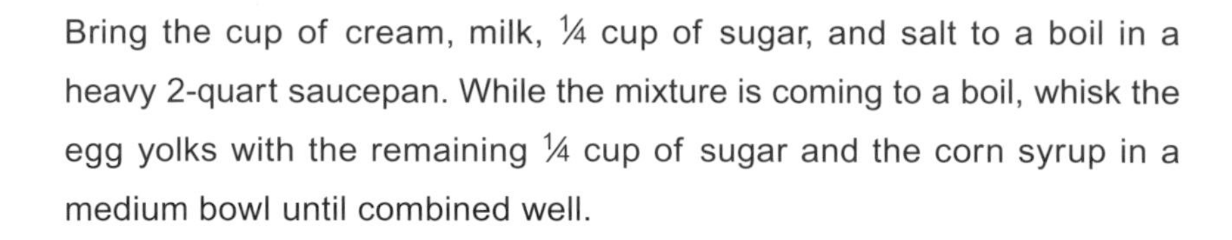

Bring the cup of cream, milk, ¼ cup of sugar, and salt to a boil in a heavy 2-quart saucepan. While the mixture is coming to a boil, whisk the egg yolks with the remaining ¼ cup of sugar and the corn syrup in a medium bowl until combined well.

When the milk mixture comes to a boil, pour one-third of it into the egg mixture, whisking constantly. Add another third and whisk again. Return the egg mixture to the pan. Reduce the heat to moderate and whisk constantly until the mixture reaches 170° F.

Remove from the heat immediately, pour through a strainer directly over the melted chocolate, and gently whisk until the chocolate is incorporated. Cool to room temperature and refrigerate for 6 hours or overnight, until the mixture is thoroughly chilled and very thick.

Make the ice cream according to the manufacturer's directions and transfer to freezer containers. Swirl in the white chocolate gently, using a rubber spatula.

Alternately, smooth one-quarter of the ice cream into a container and quickly smooth about 1 tablespoon white chocolate mixture on top. Repeat to make four layers of each and freeze for 4 hours or until firm enough to scoop.

easy ice cream concoctions

Got the urge to turn your ice-cream into another dessert entirely? Try one of these easy-to-create chocolate ice cream temptations.

Affogato

1 scoop dark chocolate ice cream (page 42)

1 shot Amaretto, Kahlua, Frangelico, or other liqueur

1 shot freshly brewed espresso

Place a medium scoop of ice cream in your favorite coffee cup and drizzle with the shot of liqueur. Pour the freshly brewed espresso over the ice cream and enjoy immediately.

Chocolate Chocolate Chip Ice Cream Sandwich

12 ounces of good quality chocolate chips

24 of your favorite homemade chocolate chip cookies (see pages 53-54)

½ gallon of dark chocolate ice cream, softened (page 38)

Spread the chocolate chips out on a plate. Place a small half-scoop of ice cream on the flat side of a cookie. Place another cookie on top of the ice-cream and press the sandwich together until the ice cream comes to the very edge. Roll the cookie sandwich in the chocolate chips to lightly coat. Place the sandwich on a cookie sheet (work quickly to finish making the rest of the sandwiches). Wrap the cookie sheet in plastic wrap and freeze for 1 hour.

Hot and Cold Chocolate

1 cup of our hot chocolate (page 138)

1 scoop of dark chocolate ice cream (page 42)

Fresh whipped cream (page 31)

Make sure your hot chocolate mug has some extra room. Gently add the scoop of ice cream to the mug and top with whipped cream.

deep dark brownies

YIELD: 9 BROWNIES

The great brownie debate never ends: cakey vs. fudgy. In our attempts to lure fans on both sides of the spectrum, we enlisted Lesli Heffler to bake a "happy medium" brownie for our store. Her brownie is neither light as air nor fudgy and underbaked; it is somewhere blissfully in between. Our customers are delighted.

¾ cup all-purpose flour
¼ teaspoon salt
1 tablespoon cocoa powder
4 ounces (1 stick) unsalted butter
¾ teaspoon instant espresso powder
5 ounces semisweet chocolate
¾ cup granulated sugar
¼ cup light brown sugar
3 large eggs
1 teaspoon vanilla extract
¾ cup (4½ ounces) semisweet chocolate chips (optional)

Preheat the oven to 350° F (see Note). Butter an 8-inch square baking pan.

Sift the flour, salt, and cocoa powder together into a bowl; set aside.

In a medium-large, heavy saucepan, combine the butter and espresso powder and stir over low heat until the butter is melted. Add the chocolate, stirring constantly until the mixture appears completely smooth, approximately 2 minutes.

Take the chocolate mixture off the heat and add the sugars, mixing until combined.

Add the eggs and vanilla and continue stirring until they are evenly incorporated and the mixture does not appear grainy.

Sprinkle the sifted flour over the mixture and stir just until blended. Stir in the chips if using.

Pour the batter into the greased pan and smooth the top. Bake the brownies for 28 to 30 minutes, or until a toothpick inserted in the center comes out with a few moist crumbs. Do not overbake. Cool completely on a wire rack.

Note: If you are using a dark-colored baking pan, reduce the oven temperature by 25 degrees.

Variation: Lime Brownies

For something different, try these in the summer.

Follow the above recipe, but omit espresso powder and substitute the juice (strained) and zest of 1 lime. Increase the amount of all-purpose flour in the recipe to 1 cup. If you like, decorate the tops of the brownies with a swirl of melted white chocolate colored with green food coloring.

when is a brownie not really a brownie?

The brownie elite are a ferocious, vocal, but entirely principled group. On behalf of this secretive society, we have collected a list of their strict rules and regulations:

- Icing on a brownie is disturbing and unnecessary. Are you trying to hide a dry, tasteless square?
- If you crave a cakey consistency, bake a cake.
- If you still insist on a cakey brownie, do not attempt to achieve this consistency by baking for an extra five minutes. This is called overbaking. It is inedible. Instead, simply add an egg or two, some flour, and a hint of baking powder and baking soda to the recipe.
- If you crave a fudgy consistency, make fudge. You should not have to spoon a cooked brownie out of the pan. This is called soup.
- If you still insist on a fudgy brownie, do not attempt to achieve this consistency by underbaking. This is called uncooked batter. Instead, remove the baking powder and baking soda and remove an egg. When beating the batter, take care not to overbeat or you will incorporate too much air, thus rendering a "cakier" variety.

This secret society's principles are stringent. However, we still prefer to heap ice-cream on top of our warm brownie and eat it while watching midnight infomercials. Needless to say, the brownie elite would not approve.

chocolate fudge layer cake

YIELD: 10 SERVINGS

In our quest for the ideal chocolate layer cake, we found it nearly impossible to improve upon the perfection of Tish Boyle's Chocolate Fudge Layer Cake. It's moist, chocolaty, and stalwart. Serve it with milk and forever be happy. This recipe appears in her book, Diner Desserts, *a must-have for your cookbook collection.*

Fudge Cake:

2⅔ cups all-purpose flour
1½ cups granulated sugar
1 cup firmly packed light brown sugar
½ cup unsweetened nonalkalized cocoa powder
2 teaspoons baking powder
1 teaspoon baking soda
½ teaspoon salt
3 large eggs, at room temperature
⅔ cup sour cream, at room temperature
1 tablespoon vanilla extract
¾ cup (1½ sticks) unsalted butter, melted and cooled
½ cup corn oil
1¼ cups ice water

Fudge Frosting:

6 ounces unsweetened chocolate
1 cup (2 sticks) unsalted butter, softened
2 cups confectioners' sugar, sifted
1 tablespoon vanilla extract

Prepare the cake:

Preheat the oven to 350° F. Butter the bottom and sides of two 8-inch round cake pans. Dust the pans with flour and tap out the excess.

In a medium bowl, sift together the flour, sugars, cocoa, baking powder, baking soda, and salt. Stir the dry ingredients together with a whisk.

In a medium bowl, whisk together the eggs, sour cream, and vanilla until blended. In the bowl of an electric mixer, using the paddle attachment or beaters, beat the melted butter and corn oil on low speed until blended. Beat in the water. Add the dry ingredients all at once and mix on low speed for about 1 minute, until blended. Scrape down the sides of the bowl with a rubber spatula. Add the egg mixture and mix for about 1 minute, or until blended. Scrape the batter into the prepared pans.

Bake the cakes for 50 to 55 minutes, or until a toothpick inserted into the center of each cake comes out clean. Cool the cakes in the pans on wire racks for 15 minutes. Invert the cakes onto the racks and cool completely.

Prepare the fudge frosting:

Put the chocolate in the top of a double boiler and melt over barely simmering water. Remove the top of the double boiler and let the chocolate cool.

In the bowl of an electric mixer, using the paddle attachment, beat the butter on medium-high speed for about 1 minute, or until creamy. Add the sifted confectioners' sugar and beat for about 2 minutes, or until well blended and light. Beat in the vanilla extract. Reduce the speed to low and beat in the cooled chocolate. Increase the speed to medium-high and beat for about 1 minute, or until glossy and smooth.

To assemble the cake:

Using a long, serrated knife, slice off the domed top of each cake layer, so that the cakes are flat. Place the cake scraps in a food processor and process for 20 seconds, until the scraps are fine crumbs. Set the crumbs aside.

Place one cake layer on a serving plate. Scrape about ½ cup of the frosting over the cake, and using a small offset metal spatula, spread it into an even layer. Top with the second cake layer. Frost the top and sides of the cake with the remaining frosting. Sprinkle the top of the cake with some of the reserved cake crumbs. Pat the remaining cake crumbs around the sides of the cake. Serve the cake immediately, or refrigerate and bring to room temperature before serving.

spiced oatmeal chocolate-chip cookies

YIELD: 20 TO 24 COOKIES

We are ever grateful to Tammy Ogletree (a.k.a. CookieChick) for providing us with our cookie recipes. The results are plump, chewy, and addictive. CookieChick has made the cookies at our store since our opening day, and they continue to sell at a rollicking pace. These are the perfect fall cookie with a cinnamon kick!

1¾ cups unbleached flour

1 teaspoon baking soda

1 teaspoon salt

1 teaspoon ground cinnamon

1 cup (2 sticks) unsalted butter, softened

1¼ cups dark brown sugar

¼ cup granulated sugar

2 eggs

2 teaspoons vanilla extract

2¾ cups organic whole oats

12 ounces bittersweet chocolate pieces (you may also use chunk chocolate, coarsely chopped)

Sift the flour, baking soda, salt and cinnamon together and set aside. In a medium-size mixing bowl, cream the butter with both sugars until smooth. Add the eggs and vanilla, beating until very fluffy. You may use an electric mixer if desired. Add the sifted ingredients, mixing thoroughly until the batter is smooth. Add the oats and chocolate, mixing until just blended. Chill the dough for at least 6 hours.

Preheat the oven to 350° F.

Drop by tablespoonfuls, about 1½ ounces each, on an ungreased baking sheet. Bake for 13 to 15 minutes. Once finished baking, allow the cookies to cool for 8 to 10 minutes before transferring to a cooling rack.

white chocolate macadamia nut cookies

YIELD: 20 TO 24 COOKIES

Here's another winning cookie recipe from Tammy Ogletree of CookieChick. Perfect for breakfast (yes, breakfast) or as an accompaniment to a cup of hot chocolate.

1 cup (2 sticks) unsalted butter
1 cup light brown sugar
¼ cup granulated sugar
2 eggs
2 teaspoons vanilla extract
2¼ cups unbleached flour
2 teaspoons salt
1 teaspoon baking soda
8 ounces macadamia nuts, coarsely chopped (you may use salted or unsalted)
8 ounces white chocolate pieces (you may also use chunk chocolate, coarsely chopped)

Sift the flour, baking soda, and salt together and set aside. In a medium-size mixing bowl, cream the butter with both sugars until smooth. Add the eggs and vanilla, beating until very fluffy. You may use an electric mixer if desired. Add the sifted ingredients, mixing thoroughly until the batter is smooth. Add the nuts and chocolate, mixing until just blended. Chill the dough for at least 6 hours.

Preheat the oven to 375° F.

Drop by tablespoonfuls (about 1½ ounces each) on an ungreased baking sheet. Be sure not to drop the cookies too close together on the baking sheet to allow room for spreading. Bake for 12 to 15 minutes. Once finished baking, allow the cookies to cool for 8 to 10 minutes before transferring to a cooling rack.

banana chocolate chip pancakes

YIELD: TWELVE TO SIXTEEN 3-INCH PANCAKES

Bananas and chocolate: This is our version of a great breakfast. Adapted from Grandma's classic banana pancake recipe (Grandma is going to be upset we eliminated the bacon fat—she makes everything with bacon fat) and tweaked to include a hint of cocoa and a handful of chocolate chips, this is an appetizing way to start your morning. This recipe is lighter and less sweet than a cookie, but much more interesting than a typical airy pancake.

2 eggs
1 cup milk
¼ cup heavy cream
2 teaspoons vanilla extract
3 tablespoons butter, melted
1½ cups unbleached flour
Dash salt
2 teaspoons baking powder
1 teaspoon good quality unsweetened cocoa powder
¾ cups bittersweet chocolate chips
1 mildly ripe banana (thinly sliced)
Extra butter to grease griddle

In a standing mixer, beat the eggs, milk, cream and vanilla on high speed for about 3 minutes or until very light and foamy. Remove mixture from the mixer and whisk in butter.

In a small bowl, sift the flour, salt, baking powder and cocoa powder together.

Pour the sifted ingredients into the egg and milk mixture and stir until just combined. Cover with plastic wrap and place batter in the refrigerator for one hour (batter can sit overnight).

Preheat and grease griddle with about 1 tablespoon of butter. Check the griddle temperature by dropping a small amount of water on the surface. If the water sizzles and evaporates immediately, your griddle is ready.

Remove pancake batter from the refrigerator and gently stir batter to loosen it up (mixture will have slightly hardened). Pour chocolate chips and thinly sliced banana into the mixture and stir until both ingredients are completely submerged in batter.

Pour about ¼ cup of batter onto the griddle and cook until the surface of the pancake is covered in tiny bubbles that begin to break. Flip pancake and cook until the second side is golden brown (about 1½ to 2 minutes) Repeat with remaining batter.

Serve pancakes fresh off the griddle with real maple syrup.

peanut butter cupcakes with chocolate ganache icing

YIELD: 18 LARGE OR 24 MEDIUM CUPCAKES

This recipe is quick, easy, and perfect for those times when a peanut-butter-and-chocolate craving sets in. It's the ideal fix!

Cupcakes:

¼ cup peanut butter (all-natural works fine)
6 tablespoons (¾ stick) unsalted butter, softened
1 teaspoon vanilla extract
1½ cups dark brown sugar
2 eggs
2 cups sifted flour
2 teaspoons baking powder
½ teaspoon salt
¾ cup milk

Chocolate Ganache Icing:

8 ounces bittersweet chocolate, coarsely chopped
1 cup heavy cream
2 tablespoons (¼ stick) unsalted butter
2 tablespoons light corn syrup

Prepare the cupcakes:

Preheat the oven to 375° F.

Line a muffin tin with paper cups.

Cream the peanut butter, butter, and vanilla in a large bowl until well mixed. Gradually add the sugar to the mixture, beating until light and fluffy, about 3 minutes. Add the eggs one at a time, beating until incorporated.

In a separate bowl, sift the flour, baking powder, and salt together. In three alternating batches, add the sifted ingredients and milk to the batter. Scrape down the sides of the bowl as needed in between additions. Beat until incorporated.

For larger cupcakes fill the paper cups until just below the rim. For medium cupcakes fill the paper cups two-thirds full.

Place in the oven and bake for 20 minutes, or until a toothpick inserted into a cupcake comes out clean. Do not overbake. Remove from the oven and cool for 10 minutes in the pan before transferring the cupcakes to wire racks to cool completely.

Prepare the icing:

Place the chocolate in a medium bowl and set aside.

In a heavy 1-quart saucepan, using a wooden spoon, combine the cream, butter, and corn syrup and cook over medium heat until hot but not boiling (little beads will form on the sides of the pot). Pour the cream over the chocolate and stir until blended. Let the ganache cool for 15 to 20 minutes.

One by one, dip the top of each peanut butter cupcake into the ganache. Let excess ganache drip off before flipping the cupcake to an upright position.

Note: Turn your ganache icing into a traditional and delicious "frosting." Once the icing has reached room temperature, cover and refrigerate for approximately 30 to 45 minutes. Remove, unwrap, and whip until creamy.

why cupcakes?

Cupcakes serve a purpose. True, some can be cute and cloying, but we'll defend their right to exist as long as they don't sacrifice anything in taste and texture. A terrible-tasting cupcake dressed up in an abundance of gorgeous decoration is still a terrible cupcake. Period.

Great-tasting cupcakes have several uses.

Cupcakes are perfect for portion control.
You might feel guilty (we wouldn't) eating a large cake slice, but scarfing a cupcake hardly feels like a sin. We don't recommend eating less than two cupcakes per sitting.

Cupcakes are created equally.
No need to fight over the largest slice, they are all the same size.

Cupcakes are portable.
Grab and eat one on the go.

There is no exact science for converting your favorite cake batter recipe to a cupcake recipe, though it is a fairly easy process. In general, you will decrease the baking time originally called for (check your cupcakes early and often) and we recommend filling the cupcake tins only half-full until you are more familiar with how much they will rise. Good luck and enjoy.

GOD BLESS AMERICA
THE LAND THAT I LOVE.

retro reconfigured

We are hopelessly retro.

We are nostalgic for things we never experienced: pies and cakes from the Automat, malteds and egg creams from the local soda jerk, and aisles and aisles of dime-store candy. History books, classic films, old magazines, and vintage cookbooks help feed our retro obsession, and through them, we celebrate these never-experienced memories.

Our retro chocolate inspirations are greatly influenced by the energy and soul of treats that came from yesteryear's boardwalks, carnivals, and state fairs. Big food. Loud food. Messy food. Lopsided banana splits drowned in lakes of chocolate. Taffy stretched from hand to mouth. Fudge the size of mountains. We strive to interpret the retro desserts with a sincere admiration and avoid the kitsch and camp that often accompanies these sweets.

The philosophy is simple: You learn from the past.

BOARDWALK INSPIRATIONS

The chocolate pioneers were born on the boardwalk, and Brooklyn's Coney Island was America's boardwalk.

Coney Island's food stalls were like the boardwalk itself, noisy and energetic, amusing and real. Chocolate was not a precious and exclusive jewel but a wild and exciting ingredient that harmonized with anything: apples, bananas, various nuts, ice cream, penny candy, popcorn, and pretzels. The chocolate was sweet. The confections were large, imperfect, and inexpensive. The customers were happy.

Philip's Candy, a Coney Island institution for seventy years, greeted sugar-starved customers the moment they left the Stillwell Avenue subway terminal. John Dorman, owner and confectionery chemist for fifty-four years, created some truly amazing chocolate treats, such as freshly dipped chocolate-covered strawberries, chocolate jelly bars, and apples bathed in rich chocolate. Everything was made by hand! No fancy machines, no electronic cash register. The interior was energetic, tiny, and without a fanciful or well-planned design—it was actually too small for customers to enter. Philip's Candy was, quite simply, a man, his sugar, his chocolate, and his loyal customers.

Sadly, Philip's Candy closed. In the spring of 2001, John Dorman served his last box of chocolate cashew clusters from his Surf Avenue address. We thank John and Philip's Candy for their inspiration and experimentation.

Boardwalks aren't like they used to be. The chocolate candy pioneers with their copper kettles and spun sugar have been replaced by faux "olde fudge and taffy shoppes" and other less appetizing chocolate peddlers. You can still find the occasional tried-and-true boardwalk stalwarts, but they are harder and harder to find.

Don't forget the lessons learned by the boardwalk: Chocolate is real. Chocolate is amusing, immediate, and messy. Chocolate is forever.

DIME-STORE CANDY LAND

Like most Americans, we grew up on mass-produced chocolate, and we are proud of it. Kit Kat's, Reese's Pieces, Hershey Kisses, and M&M's ran through our bloodstream, and the dime-store candy shop was our paradise.

We haven't entirely given up on these treats; we just eat them more sparingly. Sure, they're overly sweet and laden with additives, preservatives, and chemical components. Milk Duds can pull your fillings out,

and a Three Musketeers bar is so sweet it will make your teeth hurt, but we don't really care. We eat these down-market goodies on impulse, at the movies, when we need a boost, as a fast snack, or when we want a quick nostalgic jolt. Besides, they are damn convenient.

Though the corner candy shops are a dying breed, the Big Daddy of all penny candy stores still lives and breathes in the Big Apple. Economy Candy, Manhattan's sugar-shock emporium, has been operating since 1937. Second-generation purveyors Jerry Cohen and his wife, Ilene, run the store with a large infusion of personality. Good news: The store is not shiny and polished and antiseptically clean. Quite the contrary—the shelves, walls, and aisles of this Lower East Side institution are exploding with candy, chocolate, and color in a free-flowing hyper-rhythm. It feels as though the store itself is made out of sugar and syrup and cocoa—it's Candyland come to life.

During our many pilgrimages to this candy nirvana, we stock up on hard-to-find imports—they have a growing British chocolate candy section, nostalgic must-haves (think Mallo cups), and their famous hand-dipped pretzels in dark chocolate. Jerry and Ilene both have vast knowledge of the sweet, the chocolaty, and the sticky, so feel free to inquire about your long-lost favorite in person or online at www.economycandy.com.

We urge you to pass up those charmless, dreary chain grocery stores when you are thinking of purchasing your favorite mass-produced confection. Find your mom-and-pop sweet shop instead—the sugar is sweeter all around.

CHOCOLATE CANDY: A LOOK BACK

What's in a Name?

In a truly bizarre case of marketing brilliance (or insanity), the Sperry Candy Company of Milwaukee, Wisconsin, introduced the Chicken Dinner Candy Bar. The bar, actually a chocolate-peanut roll, contained no poultry products (thankfully!) The name and packaging aspired to evoke the satisfaction of eating a perfectly roasted chicken dinner. Hmm? The Chicken Dinner Bar disappeared when Pearson's Candy of Minneapolis purchased the Sperry Company in 1962.

Something for Everyone

The Seven Up Bar was eager to please. This candy bar was comprised of seven different chocolate pieces, each one filled with a different flavor—think of it as seven different truffles fused together. The flavors changed throughout Seven Up's life, but you could always count on a few caramels and nuts and occasionally a jelly. With a high manufacturing cost and some trademark name issues (think large soda company), the bar was retired from Pearson's in the late seventies.

A Seasonal Fever

Nabisco's decades-old Mallomar inspires a raging fervor among its devotees. Poetry, essays, recipes, and websites are all dedicated to this simple confection. The Mallomar, comprised of a graham cracker and marshmallow enrobed in chocolate (yes, it is a relative of the s'more), appears on store shelves only during the colder winter months and vanishes as the summer months approach. It's awfully fragile. To survive a Mallomarless summer, addicts buy Mallomars in enormous quantities to freeze and serve as needed. Stock up early; stores have been known to run out before the first signs of spring.

Powerful

The Powerhouse Bar was a staggering 4 ounces of fudge, peanuts, and caramel. By comparison, today's average candy bar weighs in at a measly 1.5 ounces. It was the Mount Everest of candy bars. The Walter Johnson Candy Company introduced the Powerhouse in the late twenties, and it was popular enough in the forties to sponsor comics in the Sunday newspaper. After Walter Johnson was absorbed by the Peter Paul Candy Company in the late sixties, the bar began to lose its "bigness." Slowly but surely the bar was reduced to a tiny 2 ounces, then disappeared forever when Hershey bought Peter Paul in 1988. It was a slow, painful, sad end to the most powerful bar on earth.

retro recipes

chocolate icebox cake

YIELD: 2 CAKES

Voilà, our version of the icebox cake. This recipe is fancy and fun without any of the froufrou. The chocolate ladyfingers are sure to please on their own, but they become a heavenly cake layer once paired with the fruit and mascarpone filling. Enjoy, and don't be afraid of the ingredients list; it is fairly simple to make.

Chocolate Ladyfingers:

½ cup plus 2 tablespoons cake flour, sifted

2 tablespoons plus 1 teaspoon unsweetened cocoa powder

2 eggs, separated

1 egg, whole

½ cup sugar

½ teaspoon vanilla extract

⅛ teaspoon cream of tartar

Syrup and Macerated Fruit:

¼ cup sugar

¾ cup water

1 tablespoon dark rum

2 punnets (or containers) raspberries

Mascarpone Filling:

¾ cup heavy cream

5 large egg yolks

½ cup sugar

½ cup water

16 ounces mascarpone

1 teaspoon vanilla extract

1 tablespoon dark rum

Prepare the ladyfingers:

Preheat the oven to 400° F.

Line two 12 x 17-inch baking sheets with parchment paper.

Sift together the flour and 2 tablespoons of cocoa powder three times. In a standing mixer fitted with the whisk attachment, beat the yolks, 1 egg, ¼ cup of the sugar, and the vanilla on high speed until pale and fluffy, approximately 3 minutes. Transfer the mixture to a bowl.

In a standing mixer fitted with the whisk attachment, beat the egg whites at medium speed until foamy. Add the cream of tartar and continue beating until the whites hold a very soft peak. Increase the mixer speed to high, and add the remaining ¼ cup of sugar in a steady stream. Continue to beat until the egg whites are glossy and medium stiff peaks form.

Fold half of the egg-white mixture into the egg-yolk mixture until just combined. Sprinkle in the flour mixture and the remaining whites and fold in until combined. Transfer the mixture to a pastry bag fitted with a medium plain tip. Do not overfill your pastry bag.

Pipe the mixture onto a baking sheet into 3 rectangular, zigzag patterned rows, 2½ inches wide and 6½ inches long; repeat on another baking sheet. Dust with the remaining cocoa powder and bake for 8 to 10 minutes, until the top forms a crust.

Remove from the oven and cool in the pan. Carefully peel off the parchment paper to remove the ladyfingers.

Prepare the syrup and fruit:

In a heavy 1-quart saucepan, bring the sugar and water to a boil; let boil for approximately 5 minutes. Let cool and stir in the rum.

When the mixture is cool, add 2 tablespoons of it to a large mixing bowl and reserve the remaining syrup. Add the raspberries and gently mix to coat. Allow to macerate while preparing the mascarpone filling.

Prepare the filling:

In the bowl of a standing mixer fitted with the whisk attachment, beat the cream until soft peaks form. Transfer to a small bowl and leave in the fridge to chill.

In a standing mixer fitted with the whisk attachment, beat the yolks on moderately high speed until pale and fluffy.

Boil the sugar and water in a heavy 1-quart saucepan until an instant-read thermometer registers 180° F.

Reduce the mixer speed to moderate and carefully pour the boiling sugar into the egg-yolk mixture (pour toward the sides of the bowl, avoiding the whip). Increase the speed to moderately high and mix until the egg mixture is cool (touch the exterior bottom of the bowl to check).

Using a rubber spatula, soften the mascarpone in a bowl. Add the vanilla and rum and gently mix with the egg-yolk mixture until combined. Transfer to a large mixing bowl. Fold the heavy cream into the egg mixture until incorporated.

Assemble the cake:

Line two 3½ x 7½ x 2½-inch loaf pans with plastic wrap, leaving a 5-inch border hanging over the edges on the long sides. Center a chocolate ladyfinger along the bottom layer of each loaf pan with the cocoa side (top side) down. Using a pastry brush, generously brush some syrup on the chocolate ladyfingers after they have been placed in the mold.

Spread ⅓ cup of mascarpone cream on top and smooth with a spatula. Evenly sprinkle ½ cup of raspberries on top, place a second layer of chocolate ladyfingers, cocoa sides (top sides) down, in the center, and press gently to even out. Repeat with mascarpone cream and the remaining raspberries. Place a final layer of chocolate ladyfingers, cocoa sides (top sides) down. Gently press down until the chocolate ladyfingers are even with the cream.

Bring up the sides of the plastic wrap and fold to seal. Chill overnight.

Note: If you have leftover mascarpone cream, you can reserve it for the top layer once you unmold the cake.

To serve:

Unfold the plastic wrap and open to expose the cake. Invert a serving plate on top of the mold. Turn over to invert the plate and mold and tap the sides of the mold gently to release the cake. Carefully remove the remaining plastic wrap. Dust with cocoa powder.

Serve sliced with additional fresh berries or sliced stone fruit (peaches, plums, cherries) sprinkled with some chopped fresh mint and sugar.

chocolate peanut butter sandwich cookies

by Chef Nick Malgieri

YIELD: ABOUT 18 COOKIES, DEPENDING ON THE SIZE OF THE CUTTER USED

We are forever indebted to Nick Malgieri for his book, Chocolate. *Each of our copies of the book are dog-eared, butter-stained, and perpetually in use. He has been very helpful to us in providing feedback on all of our chocolate inquiries (a.k.a. emergencies) and we are so happy to have him contribute to this book.*

These delicate, crumbly, chocolate cookie bases are sandwiched with a buttery peanut butter filling, making a great new variation on that classic flavor combination. Make sure to use semisweet chocolate for the cookies. Since there's no added sugar in the dough, with a darker chocolate the cookies themselves would not be sweet enough.

Cookie Dough:

12 tablespoons (1½ sticks) unsalted butter, very soft
4 ounces semisweet chocolate, melted and cooled
1¾ cups all-purpose flour

Peanut Butter Filling:

4 tablespoons (½ stick) unsalted butter, softened
¼ smooth peanut butter
1 cup confectioners' sugar
1 teaspoon vanilla extract

Prepare the dough:

Beat the butter in a bowl with a rubber spatula until creamy. Stir in the chocolate, then flour, continuing to stir until a soft dough forms. Scrape the dough onto a piece of plastic wrap and press it out thinly. Cover with more plastic wrap and refrigerate until cold and firm.

Prepare the filling:

While the dough is chilling, make the filling. Beat the butter and peanut butter in the bowl of an electric mixer or by hand, until soft and smooth. Add the sugar and vanilla and continue to beat for a few minutes or until the filling has a fluffy consistency. Reserve covered.

When you are ready to bake the cookies, set racks in the upper and lower thirds of the oven and preheat to 350° F.

Roll the dough on a floured surface (pound and knead it lightly first if it is very hard) to a thickness of 3⁄16 inch. Use a fluted 2-inch cutter to make the cookies.

Place the cut-out cookies an inch apart all around on two cookie sheets or jelly roll pans, lined with parchment or foil. Re-roll the scraps to make more cookies.

Bake the cookies for about 12 to 15 minutes, or until they are firm when pressed with a fingertip. Cool the cookies on the pans on racks.

To fill in cookies, arrange half of them flat side up on one of the pans. Pipe or spread a dab of filling in the center of each. Top with the remaining cookies, flat side down, pressing gently to make the filling come to the edge of the cookie.

double fudge

YIELD: ONE 8-INCH SQUARE

Fudge is often ignored and lonely—the forgotten chocolate dessert. It rarely receives the five-star treatment, too often being manufactured as a grainy, too-sweet confection in places with names like Ye Olde Fudge Shoppe. We intend to bring fudge to the forefront again with this melt-in-your-mouth recipe. We love the taste and visual combination of these fudges; feel free, however, to make either one as an individual dessert.

A few suggestions before you start:

- *This is an easy process but involves the use of a thermometer and requires attention to temperature, as crystallization is necessary to achieve a creamy fudge consistency.*

- *We recommend using a stand mixer.*

- *Unnecessary stirring will make your fudge grainy.*

- *It may take one or two tries to get it right, but the result will be true fudge, well worth the effort of making it yourself.*

White Chocolate Walnut Fudge:

1 cup walnuts or pecans, chopped

2 cups sugar

¾ cup half-and-half

2 tablespoons dark corn syrup

¼ teaspoon salt

8 ounces white chocolate chips

2 tablespoons unsalted butter, softened

1 teaspoon vanilla extract

Dark Chocolate Fudge:

2 cups sugar

¾ cup half-and-half

2 tablespoons light corn syrup

¼ teaspoon salt

4 ounces bittersweet chocolate, chopped fine

2 tablespoons unsalted butter, softened

1 teaspoon vanilla extract

½ cup walnuts or pecans (optional; reserved from preceding recipe)

Prepare the White Chocolate Walnut Fudge:

Preheat oven to 350° F. Spread the nuts in a single layer on a baking sheet and toast until golden, about 10 minutes. Set aside half for the white chocolate fudge and half for the dark fudge.

Line an 8 x 8-inch heatproof dish with foil and lightly coat with butter.

In a heavy 2-quart saucepan over moderate heat, dissolve the sugar, half-and-half, corn syrup, salt, and half (4 ounces) of the white chocolate chips. Whisk until smooth and do not stir further. Bring to a boil until a thermometer registers 240° F (about 8 to 10 minutes). Pour into a heat-proof bowl and add the butter and vanilla but do not stir. Allow to cool to 110° F undisturbed, about 1 hour.

Transfer to a standing mixer fitted with the paddle attachment and mix on low speed until a dull matte look appears on the surface, about 15 minutes. (The mixture will be glossy at first, then thicken and become dull. If the mixture becomes too thick, thin it with a few drops of heavy cream or half-and-half.) Mix in the remaining half (4 ounces) of the white chocolate chips, transfer to the prepared pan, and smooth the top with a spatula. Sprinkle the top with ½ cup of nuts and refrigerate.

While the White Chocolate Walnut Fudge sets, prepare the Dark Chocolate Fudge layer:

Prepare the Dark Chocolate Fudge:

In a heavy 2-quart saucepan over moderate heat, dissolve the sugar, half-and-half, corn syrup, salt, and chocolate. Whisk until smooth and do not stir further. Bring to a boil until a thermometer registers 240° F (about 8 to 10 minutes). Pour into a heatproof bowl and add the butter and vanilla but do not stir. Allow to cool to 110° F undisturbed, about 1 hour.

Transfer to a standing mixer fitted with the paddle attachment and mix on low speed until a dull matte look appears on the surface, about 15 minutes. The mixture will be glossy at first, then thicken and become dull. (If the mixture becomes too thick, thin it with a few drops of heavy cream or half-and-half.) Smooth on top of the White Chocolate Walnut Fudge with a spatula. Sprinkle the top with the reserved ½ cup of nuts.

Refrigerate for 2 hours or until firm.

Remove the fudge from the pan and peel off the foil. Cut with a heavy sharp knife into neat squares or any shape you like. (Running the knife blade under hot water and wiping it dry makes for clean, straight edges.)

amazing chocolate malted

YIELD: 1 EXTRA-LARGE SERVING OR
2 SMALL SERVINGS

Behold the amazing malted, staple of soda-shop nostalgia. It's thick, rich, and creamy. (Most supermarkets carry malt powder near the hot chocolate mix section.)

2 tablespoons Chocolate Syrup (see recipe below)
2 large scoops chocolate ice cream
¾ cup milk
½ cup ice
1 tablespoon malt powder

Place all of the ingredients in a blender and mix until smooth.

Chocolate Syrup

YIELD: 2 CUPS

The syrup can be made ahead of time and kept in the refrigerator. It can also be served over ice cream or pound cake.

1 cup water
¾ cup sugar
½ cup unsweetened cocoa powder
½ cup heavy cream

Bring the water and sugar to a boil in a 1-quart saucepan. Whisk together the cocoa and cream, add to the saucepan and bring to a boil. Pour through a fine-mesh sieve and cool to room temperature.

colossal chocolate sundae mountain

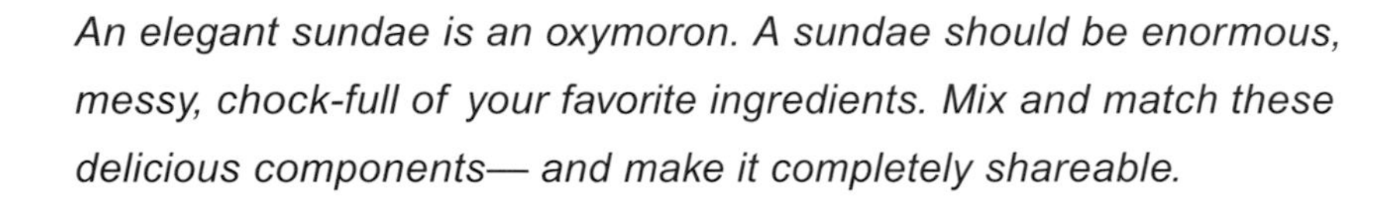

An elegant sundae is an oxymoron. A sundae should be enormous, messy, chock-full of your favorite ingredients. Mix and match these delicious components— and make it completely shareable.

Dark Chocolate Ice Cream with White Chocolate Swirl (see page 38), or your preferred flavor of premium store-bought ice cream
Deep Dark Brownies (see page 42)
Gingered Walnuts, Hazelnuts, or Almonds (recipe follows)
Minted Chocolate Sauce (see page 145)
Vanilla Whipped Cream (recipe follows)
Fresh berries

Gingered Walnuts, Hazelnuts, or Almonds:

YIELD: 1¼ CUPS

¼ cup light brown sugar
½ teaspoon ground ginger
1 cup walnuts or hazelnuts, chopped, or almonds, whole
2 teaspoons egg white
2 teaspoons corn syrup
½ tablespoon unsalted butter

Preheat the oven to 375° F and place an oven rack in the middle position. Spread the nuts out in a thin layer on a baking sheet and bake until lightly toasted, about 10 minutes.

While the nuts are toasting, rub the brown sugar with the ginger by hand until combined in a medium mixing bowl. Add the remaining ingredients and whisk until well combined. Add the warm nuts to the mixture and mix with a heatproof spatula or wooden spoon until the nuts are well coated.

Spread the nuts in a single layer, as separated as possible, on a lightly buttered nonstick baking sheet. Bake in the middle position for 10 to 12 minutes, until golden.

Cool and keep in an airtight container. Nuts will keep for at least 2 weeks.

Vanilla Whipped Cream:

YIELD: 3 CUPS

¼ vanilla bean, 1 teaspoon vanilla paste (see page 188 for where to buy), or 1 teaspoon vanilla extract
¼ cup sugar
2 cups heavy cream

Split the vanilla bean, if using, and scrape the seeds using a small knife. Rub the vanilla seeds with the sugar and sprinkle into very cold heavy cream. If using vanilla paste or vanilla extract, mix with sugar into very cold heavy cream. Whisk until stiff peaks form and keep chilled.

How to Assemble Your Ice Cream Mountain:

There are no instructions per se; build your own ice cream mountain as you see fit. If you need a little guidance, feel free to follow our colossal sundae instructions:

1. Get a big, big bowl.
2. Start with a brownie as your base.
3. Place four small softened half-scoops of ice cream in each corner and sprinkle with a few gingered nuts.
4. Place another brownie on top of the ice cream, almost as if you were making a brownie-ice cream sandwich.
5. Top your second brownie with two extra-large helpings of ice cream and again, sprinkle with a few gingered nuts.
6. Finish off with a river of minted hot chocolate sauce, fresh vanilla whipped cream, and fresh berries.
7. Share this dessert.

better-than-tootsie taffy

YIELD: ABOUT 5 DOZEN CANDIES (1 POUND)

Taffy is so much fun to make alone or with a partner. You'll have a great time pulling and stretching, but the trick is to begin pulling taffy as soon as it is cool enough to handle and continue until it reaches room temperature. It's not hard to make but involves boiling hot sugar, so be sure to have a heatproof surface to work on and clean latex gloves to help protect your hands.

A bag of wrapped taffies makes a wonderful gift.

2 tablespoons unsalted butter, plus additional for greasing
⅓ cup good-quality Dutch-process cocoa powder
¾ cup water
1½ cups sugar
1 cup light corn syrup
1 teaspoon white vinegar
1 teaspoon baking soda
¼ teaspoon salt
Confectioners' sugar for dusting

Line a heavy baking sheet (with sides, not a cookie sheet) with a heatproof silicone mat, or grease generously with butter. Lay the sheet on a heatproof surface.

In a medium bowl, whisk together the cocoa powder and water until the mixture thickens, then pour through a mesh strainer into a heavy 4- to 6-quart pot. Add the sugar, corn syrup, butter, vinegar, baking soda, and salt and whisk to combine. The mixture should not fill more than half the pot as it will boil and rise during cooking. Boil over moderate heat, stirring occasionally during the first 5 to 10 minutes (when mixture is foamy), then do not stir (mixture will bubble vigorously, but settle in the pot). Continue cooking until an instant-read thermometer registers 250° F (about 15 to 20 minutes), stir in 2 tablespoons of butter until combined, and carefully pour into the prepared pan without scraping the pot. Remove from the heat.

Using a lightly buttered metal pastry scraper or a wooden spoon, begin to fold the cooler edges of taffy onto the center. (The taffy will become firmer on the edges after a few minutes, but the heat will be concentrated in the center.) Taffy will be very soft initially and seem like a thick liquid. Avoid scraping the bottom of the pan.

When the taffy is still hot but cool enough to handle, butter your gloved palms generously and gather the taffy mass in your hands (you may need to use the scraper to help you). Begin to "pull" taffy in an even thickness by stretching the mass about 1 foot apart in both hands. (Taffy may seem very soft and sticky.) Bring both ends of taffy back to each other to form a loop and pull, stretching your arms slightly. Twist the end if you like and bring it back to the top. Taffy may feel very soft at first, but it will begin to get harder to pull. Continue pulling until the taffy is lighter in color and has a satin-matte sheen (it will look somewhat like rope) but remains soft and pliable, about 10 minutes (temperature and humidity may vary and can take longer).

When it cools to room temperature, transfer to a clean cutting board and divide into quarters using large heavy shears or a heavy knife. Dust lightly with sifted confectioners' sugar, roll or stretch the taffy into a log about ¾ inch wide, and cut into ¾-inch-long pieces. If knife or scissors become sticky, grease blades with butter. Wrap each piece of taffy in waxed paper and store in an airtight container. The taffies will stay fresh for 1 week in a container.

the chocolate jiggle

YIELD: 4 SERVINGS

Gelatin? Unusual but delicious. Trust us. Dip a spoon into this shiny and attractive dessert and you will be hooked. The coffee sauce lends a nice balance to the chilled chocolate.

Espresso sauce:

1 large egg yolk

2 tablespoons sugar

¾ cup milk

1 teaspoon instant espresso granules

1 large egg yolk

Gelatin:

1½ cups water

2½ teaspoons (1 packet) powdered gelatin

½ cup heavy cream

⅓ cup sugar

¼ cup good-quality Dutch-process cocoa powder

Prepare the sauce:

With a whisk, whip the yolk and 1 tablespoon of sugar in a medium bowl until well combined.

In a heavy 1-quart saucepan, mix together the milk, remaining 1 tablespoon of sugar, and espresso granules and bring to a boil. Pour one-third of the milk mixture into the yolks, whisking constantly. Return the egg-yolk mixture to the pan and cook over moderate heat, stirring constantly, until thick enough to coat the back of a wooden spoon. Pour through a mesh strainer and cool to room temperature; then chill, covered.

Prepare the gelatin:

Pour ½ cup of water into a medium bowl and sprinkle the gelatin on top.

In a heavy 2-quart saucepan, whisk together the remaining 1 cup of water, heavy cream, sugar, and cocoa powder and bring just to a boil, stirring gently (the mixture will thicken and rise when it boils). Remove from the heat and pour into the gelatin mixture, gently stirring to combine.

Cool to room temperature and divide evenly into cups (pour about ½ cup into each). Cover with plastic wrap and chill for at least 3 hours, or until set.

This dessert can be eaten directly from the cups or prepared as a mold. If you choose to unmold the gelatin, grease the insides of the cups with vegetable oil before pouring the mixture in. To unmold, run a sharp knife against the sides of the mold to gently separate the filling. Invert a serving plate on top of the cup and invert both plate and cup in one motion. Shake slightly to loosen if necessary and unmold (it may take a few tries).

Spoon chilled espresso sauce right over the dessert in the cup or around the unmolded gelatin.

egg cream

YIELD: ONE 16-OUNCE DRINK

No, there are no eggs in an egg cream, but there is chocolate syrup. Don't bother creating your own chocolate syrup from scratch, as it would be sacrilege to use anything other than Brooklyn's own Fox's U-bet for your syrup in this recipe.

Fox's U-bet Chocolate Syrup
Milk
Seltzer

For best results use a chilled 16-ounce glass

Spoon or pour 2 inches of Fox's U-bet Chocolate Syrup into a 16-ounce glass. Add 2 inches of cold milk. Pour seltzer over a spoon to make a thick chocolaty froth. Stir and drink. Yum!

Note: It is always best to prepare an egg cream using a pressurized cylinder. As most of us don't own one nowadays and seltzer delivery men are nearly extinct, a fresh bottle of seltzer will do the job. Whatever you do, make sure it is fresh. Flat seltzer will ruin a good egg cream.

the inconclusive and often mangled history of the egg cream

What follows is a quick and humble account of the "History of the Egg Cream." It should be noted that we are neither esteemed historians nor credentialed anthropologists; we are just relaying the oft repeated and oft disputed account of the history of this native New York icon.

According to folklore, candy-store owner Louis Auster of Brooklyn made the first egg creams in 1890. These soda fountain miracles sold for three cents each, and he sold up to three thousand per day during the grueling summer heat. Egg creams were so popular in Brooklyn that author Elliot Willensky wrote "a candy store minus an egg cream, in Brooklyn at least, was as difficult to conceive of as the Earth without gravity."

As you can see from our recipe, egg creams contain neither eggs nor cream, yet the original concoction contained both. The eggs were used to create a frothy foam and the cream was added to make the drink rich and smooth. Somewhere along the line the two ingredients were dropped due to escalating ingredient costs, but the name stuck and continues to live on. Of course, this version of events has been disputed, but it is our favorite theory.

The egg cream is still a truly regional "cuisine." Step outside the five boroughs of New York City and you'd be hard pressed to find an egg cream, or even find somebody who knows what one is. But ask a New Yorker where to get the best egg cream and they'll point you towards their favorite diner, newsstand or, of course, Chocolate Bar.

peanut butter perfect pie

by Chef Andrew Shotts of Garrison Confections

YIELD: ONE 9-INCH PIE

Our good friend, chef Andrew Shotts, creates the types of chocolate confections that people line up for. Some of our customers are so devoted to his salted caramel bonbons, dark fruit-and-nut bars, and mint thins that they have asked to be notified of each and every delivery. We refer to these people as his Chocolate Stalkers.

We believe Drew has created another chocolate dessert worth stalking. His Peanut Butter Perfect Pie is addictive. From the extra-crisp crust to the three layers of beautiful filling, you won't be able to stop yourself from eating at least two slices.

Crust:

¼ cup light corn syrup

⅓ cup sugar

¼ cup plus 2 teaspoons water

¼ cup plus 2 tablespoons unsalted butter, at room temperature

2 cups plus 3 tablespoons Rice Krispies

Filling:

¾ cup peanut butter

⅔ cup milk chocolate (38% cacao), chopped

Ganache:

½ cup heavy cream

4 teaspoons light corn syrup

⅓ cup dark chocolate (61% cacao), chopped

¼ cup dark chocolate (72% cacao), chopped

¼ cup (½ stick) unsalted butter

½ cup salted peanuts

Meringue:

½ cup plus 10 tablespoons sugar

10 teaspoons water

¼ cup egg whites

¼ cup salted peanuts

Prepare the crust:

Combine the corn syrup, sugar, and water in a saucepan and cook over medium heat to a light-colored caramel. Pour the melted butter into the saucepan and add the Rice Krispies. Press into a 9-inch pie pan.

Prepare the filling:

Melt the chocolate and allow to cool to body temperature (98.6° F). Add the milk chocolate to the peanut butter and spread onto the pie crust.

Prepare the ganache:

Combine the heavy cream and the corn syrup in a saucepan and bring to a boil. Place all of the chocolate in a medium bowl and pour the cream mixture over it. Stir until combined. When it has reached body temperature (98.6° F), add the butter. Spread on top of the peanut butter layer. Place salted peanuts on top of the ganache.

Prepare the meringue:

Combine the sugar and water in a saucepan and cook to 234° F. In a standing mixer, whip the whites to a soft peak and pour the sugar mixture slowly into the whites while it is still whipping. Spread the meringue onto the ganache and garnish with the salted peanuts. For a more dramatic effect, brown the top with a propane torch before you add the peanuts.

creamy chocolate kahlua pie

YIELD: ONE 9-INCH PIE

It's easy to go from the perfect pudding to the perfect pie in these easy steps. The filling is as light and pure as a cloud and the crust provides a perfect chocolate snap. This is a 1950s inspiration, so make sure to go overboard on the fresh whipped cream and feel free to add mounds of chocolate curls (page 163).

Crust:

6 tablespoons (¾ stick) unsalted butter, melted
2 teaspoons sugar
1½ cups finely ground chocolate wafer cookies

Filling:

1 recipe of Johnny Walker Black Pudding (Page 30) with the following substitutions:
Substitute 3 tablespoons plus 1 teaspoon cornstarch for the 2 tablespoons cornstarch
Substitute 3 tablespoons Kahlua for the 3 tablespoons Johnny Walker Black

Kahlua Whipped Cream:

Follow the recipe on page 31 and add 1 tablespoon Kahlua when it calls for extract

Prepare the crust:

Preheat oven to 325°F. Butter a 9-inch pie dish.

Stir the sugar into the melted butter. Pour the butter mixture over finely-ground chocolate wafer cookies until crumbs are evenly moistened. Use your hands to press mixture into bottom and up the sides of the pie dish. Bake crust until set, about 10 minutes. Set crust aside to cool to room temperature.

Prepare the filling:

Prepare one recipe for Johnny Walker Black Pudding with substitutions. After the pudding has cooled for ten minutes, pour into prepared crust, cover with plastic wrap (wrap should come in contact with filling) and chill for at least 4 hours or overnight.

Prepare the Whipped Cream and serve:

Immediately before serving, prepare the whipped cream topping and spoon onto the pie. Slice and serve.

chocolate soufflé tart

by Chef Ilene C. Shane of SweetBliss

YIELD: ONE 10-INCH TART

Chef Ilene C. Shane is a genius at reconfiguring the sweets of another era. At our shop, she creates chocolate-encrusted jewels that ooze marshmallow, peanut butter, and caramel—each bite a study in messy chocolate perfection. This recipe is no different; the warm chocolate filling will spill out onto your plate in a gooey river. Not in the mood for ooze? Refrigerate the tart and eat chilled.

Pate Brisse (basic pie crust):

2½ cups all-purpose flour

1 teaspoon salt

½ cup sugar

2 sticks unsalted butter in small pieces (8 ounces)

¼ to ½ cup ice water

Chocolate Filling:

4 jumbo eggs, lightly beaten

½ cup flour

1½ cups sugar

1 teaspoon vanilla

½ teaspoon salt

8 ounces high-quality chocolate, chopped (bittersweet)

1½ sticks unsalted butter

½ cup of heavy cream

Prepare the pie crust:

Mix all of the dry ingredients in the bowl of a food processor, then add the cold butter and pulse until the mixture resembles coarse meal. Add the ice water slowly until the mixture comes together into a ball. Remove

from the processor and form a disk. Wrap in waxed paper and let rest in the refrigerator for 20 minutes.

Flour a work table and roll out the dough to a ⅛-inch thickness. Place in a 10-inch pie plate or ceramic tart dish. Chill the dough in the pie plate for 15 minutes.

Preheat oven to 375°–400° F. Line the pie crust with aluminum foil and weigh down with pie-weights or dry beans, covering all the corners. Bake until the edges start to brown (approximately 15 minutes), then remove the beans and foil, and bake for another 15 minutes, or until the entire crust begins to turn a golden-brown color. Remove from the oven and cool to room temperature.

Prepare the filling:

Mix the beaten eggs, flour, sugar, vanilla, and salt in a bowl. Melt the chocolate, butter, and cream in a double boiler until smooth, then mix into the egg mixture. Pour into the cooled pie crust. Bake at 350° F for 45 to 60 minutes on the middle rack. Let cool and serve with fresh whipped cream.

which is which and what is what: the tart and the pie

In a simplified world, the tart and the pie would each have exact and easy definitions, but that would make our world a terribly boring place to eat. Pies and tarts each have their own distinct personalities, but there are many cross-breeds, hybrids, and distant cousins of each term.

Defining each term is a bit daunting, because it is sure to cause debate. We have seen friendships almost end over the correct and authentic definition of "pizza" and "doughnut;" disputes that continue to this day.

With that warning, we will attempt to provide you with some quick basics:

- What makes a pie a pie? Generally speaking, a pie is baked in a pie pan or pie dish (glass, metal, or ceramic) that has sloping sides. A pie dough is usually light and flaky (though this is not always so) and is cut and served directly from the pie dish.

- So what is a Tart? The tart is usually baked in a metal pan with a removable bottom. Once the tart has been baked and assembled, the tart is removed from the pan. Therefore, the tart dough/crust has to be strong enough (i.e. not as flaky as a pie) to stand on its own.

- Both pies and tarts contain fillings as various as chocolate, custards, and fruit.

swank stuff

Chocolate is the party!

It's the slightly sweet, slightly bitter, slightly caffeinated, and completely legal party enhancer.

This is not a substance that should be treated with reserve. Chocolate is not an ending. It is not just a dessert served after the guests have sated themselves on endless bowls of chips and dips and uninspired canapés. Instead, chocolate is a beginning, a middle, and an end. It deserves prominence in appetizers, drinks, main courses, and desserts.

Remember: A party is just a party, but a chocolate party is a swank event.

THE GROOVE IS IN THE MARTINI GLASS

When we first opened Chocolate Bar in New York's West Village, we made a conscious effort to serve all of our cold chocolate drinks in a martini glass. Why? Because people like the shape. People like to hold them. And everybody loves to drink out of them. They're fun, they're sexy, and drinks look great in them.

Having a party? You'd better have some martini glasses on hand. Not serving alcohol? You'd still better have some martini glasses on hand. Fill them up with chocolate martinis and pass them out as your guests come in. Load them up with chocolate pudding and whipped cream, then top with chocolate shavings for a fun dessert. Add water and floating candles, and place them on your table for the perfect centerpiece.

Actually, it doesn't matter what you put in them; just make sure you have a lot of them around for a party.

What about a shot glass? Good, but not as flexible. How about a pilsner? Beer only, please. Champagne flute? Now you're trying too hard.

Really, trust us. We've done all of the experimenting for you. You want your party to move? You want your guests to think you're the best host ever? You want party conversation to be fluid and oh-so-interesting? There is no hidden secret, there is no magic powder, it is just as simple as this: The groove is in the martini glass.

CHOCOLATE, THE LIFE OF THE PARTY

In our continual effort to elevate chocolate to the status it deserves—playboy bon vivant—we have organized two classic theme parties with chocolate as the star. These are not party "blueprints," so feel free to improvise and add and subtract—just don't go light on the chocolate.

Pool Party BBQ

THE SETTING

The pool party barbecue is a laid-back affair; you need only a pool (aboveground, in-ground, or kiddie will do), a barbeque (charcoal or gas is fine), and some sultry weather. Want to add just a few simple, inexpensive, and attractive accoutrements? String paper lanterns through trees and around fences. Make sure citronella candles are on each and every table—they smell great, they keep the bugs away, and everyone looks better by candlelight—along with festive tableware. Offer paper fans to each guest—it's so very dramatic and charming at the same time. Oh, and dress should, of course, be casual. It's a barbecue, not a polo match!

ICE YOUR CHOCOLATE

During the summer swelter, cool down your guests with a crisp and icy chocolate drink. Set up your iced chocolate "bar" with a few martini

shakers, a blender, and margarita glasses. Set one pitcher of chilled espresso and one pitcher of chilled hot chocolate (page 138) on a bowl of ice, and have iced hot chocolate ice cubes at the ready to create a variety of shakers for your guests (page 141). For those craving the truly decadent, set aside some ice cream (page 42) or frozen yogurt and blend up malteds and milkshakes. Serve everything in a margarita or martini glass with the rim dipped in cocoa, and top everything with whipped cream. Little drink umbrellas are not necessary but highly recommended.

FIRE IT UP

The grill is the eye candy, the center of attention. Surround it with hearty condiments, thick paper plates, and heaps of napkins. Give some glory to mustard and ketchup by freeing them from their bottles and placing

them in mini bowls with deep serving spoons. Encourage your guests to swing by the grill for mounds of Spiced Cocoa Meatballs (page 124) and pigs-in-a-blanket. We can't resist festive toothpicks (barbecues warrant the use of the colorful tasseled cellophane kind) when serving finger foods—place them in any food that circulates at the party. Remember: It's easier to socialize with "mini foods," and people will have more room for dessert.

THE MIGHTY MINI

Keeping with the fit-it-all-in-your-mouth-at-once theme, top off your pool party and barbecue with Shiny Chocolate-Orange Tartlettes (page 134). Create mini tartlette pyramids by stacking them high on dinner plates and placing them poolside on cocktail tables. Decorate your tartlette tower plates with sliced oranges to add color (and vitamin C) to your single-serving dessert. Make enough for each guest to have one pre- and post-swim. We guarantee you'll hear lots of "oooh's!" and "aaah's!" by your very impressed and happily fed guests.

SCOTT

Ski Lodge Swank

THE SETTING

Thankfully, the ski-lodge setting has not been corrupted too much over the years. At almost any and every watering hole in the typical ski town, there is bound to be #1) a fireplace, #2) a bearskin rug (fakes or other animal hides work just fine), and #3) rows of beer steins. These are the only three items we suggest you provide when creating your own wintry ambience.

HOT CHOCOLATE BAR

Drinks are always the first course. As your guests arrive, offer them a full stein of steaming hot chocolate and steer them toward the hot chocolate (page 138) add-on station. The station is easy to create—simply arrange a table or bar area with big bowls of fresh vanilla whipped cream, trays overflowing with marshmallows, a bottle of peppermint schnapps or brandy, a ramekin of ground cinnamon, and a plate of candy canes for stirring. Do you have an espresso machine handy? If so, set it up beside the add-on station so guests can add a shot of buzz to their hot chocolate. Encourage your guests to come back for refills and another hot

chocolate combination. Important note: Sugar and alcohol promote a party atmosphere.

SPICE IT UP

It's time to circulate your Mole Skewers (page 128). Toothpicks are a must, as are heavy-duty napkins—no need to waste plates at this point. Pour extra mole sauce in ramekins and place throughout the party in easy-to-reach places—some guests will want their appetizers soaking with extra mole. Offer variety. Prepare a second "extra-spicy" mole (page 130), and place it in a second set of clearly labeled ramekins alongside your "mild" mole sauce.

FONDNESS FOR FONDUE

Pass out color-coded fondue forks and guide people to the fondue pots (one per table of six, please). For the friends who have reached their liquor limit and for the alcohol averse, there should be at least one chocolate fondue (page 118) pot where the alcohol is omitted. Please label this pot clearly. Heaps of accompaniments should surround each pot. Breads, fruits, marshmallows, cinnamon pastry straws, mint leaves, fresh pound cake, and just about anything the heart desires can be offered for dipping. Just make sure to have a lot on hand. Skiing is a calorie-consuming activity.

THE LAST COURSE

We normally wouldn't say this, but in this particular swank case, go easy on dessert. An icy glass of milk and Spiced Oatmeal Chocolate-Chip Cookies (page 53) are the perfect accompaniment to a roaring fire. The cookies also work well dunked in spiked hot chocolate.

TASTINGS

The art of chocolate tasting is often an all-too-serious and formal affair—but it doesn't have to be. At Chocolate Bar, tastings have proven fairly easy and inexpensive to produce. It's hard to go wrong when talking about and serving chocolate. There's no need to approach any tasting, especially a chocolate tasting, with a thick air of snobbish sophistication. Free your mind of such overused and mildly annoying terms as "bouquet"

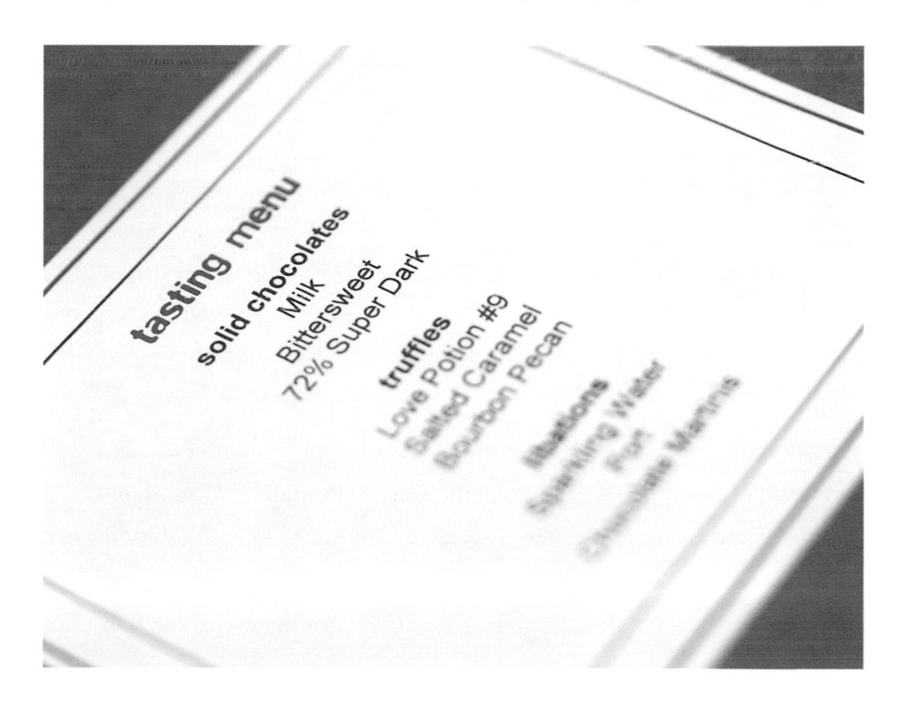

or “delicate flavor,” and the insidious “earthy undertones.” Better to chow down on a Snickers and guzzle boxed wine (we really do like some boxed wines—go figure) than endure a stiff, formal academic setting, nibbling on chocolate crumbs before the Great Cacao Scholar. Just relax, sit back, and enjoy—you will find your flavor.

Three keys to a great chocolate tasting:

Rule #1: Start with good, fresh chocolate.

There is too much good chocolate in this world to waste your time with stale or old fare. Make sure the chocolate for the tasting is purchased well before its expiration date, and make sure it hasn't bloomed (turned white).

Rule #2: Avoid any flavor-infused chocolates or truffles.

Although wasabi-roasted-onion chocolate sounds like fun, leave the wild flavors for later. Use only pure chocolate for the tasting.

Rule #3: Get a decent variety.

Milk chocolate, dark chocolate, white chocolate, single-origin chocolate, cheap chocolate, expensive chocolate, Belgian chocolate, American chocolate, French chocolate—you get the idea. After a few tastings, you can begin to narrow the field to your liking (e.g. only single-origin chocolates from Africa, or our favorite, embarrassingly bad chocolate from around the world).

A group chocolate tasting is really a simple endeavor, requiring only chocolate (obviously!); spirits, sparkling water, or both; good company; and an appropriate soundtrack.

Below are the Chocolate Bar Tasting Party suggestions. Feel free to use and abuse them:

- Invite your friends. A good, comfortable tasting should include no more than twenty chums (intimacy rules). If you have any friends who don't like chocolate, find new friends.

- Keep it cool—you need a space where everyone has a seat (no buffets, please) and a space that is not too warm—chocolate melts, after all.

- We suggest red wine and port over any other alcoholic beverages. Yes, of course you can offer beer and wine coolers, just don't invite us. Oh, and keep

chocolate tasting variations

Feeling brave? Want to narrow the focus of your chocolate-tasting party? Here are a few of our favorite variations:

The dark chocolate tasting

This is a fairly strict tasting. Concentrate on one brand or use several different brands of chocolate with a cacao content between 58% and 72%. Can you tell the subtle differences between the brands? Which one is smoother than the other? Can you tell the difference between a 60% and 72%? Can your guests?

Around-the-world chocolate tasting:

Stick to one minimal range of cacao content and sample a bite from each country. Dress up each plate in the nation's colors. Which country gets gold and which country loses miserably?

A-walk-down-memory-lane chocolate tasting:

Buy some retro chocolate, cut into slivers, hide the labels and serve. Do your guests know what they are eating? Does it bring back memories?

Unusual and terrible chocolate tasting:

This is not so much a tasting as it is a hunt. Give your friends a week's notice to find the most truly deplorable and unusual chocolate in a variety of categories. Who can find the worst flavor? Who can find the worst packaging? Who can find the worst idea in molded chocolate?

the alcohol handy and near at hand for your guests at all times throughout the evening.

- You are not a tenth-grade history professor. Tell your crowd about the fun and bizarre chocolate facts, and keep the clinical and academic information to a minimum—too much can completely kill the atmosphere. Remember, you are throwing a shindig, not hosting a lecture.

- Make sure your chocolate is chopped into bite-sized pieces. You don't want anyone to be full after the first taste. Should people attempt to have more than one bite-sized piece per chocolate, simply smack their hand. (Oh, who are we kidding? We wholeheartedly encourage chocolate gorging.)

- Passing the chocolate works best. Each kind of chocolate should have its own plate or platter and be labeled appropriately with some basic info. You can either pass the chocolate after a brief introduction or you can swank it up and hire servers.

- Did we already mention to keep the wine and port nearby and always at the ready?

a brief encounter with cacao content

cacao (ka-ka'o) *n.* A tropical tree from the seeds of which cocoa and chocolate are made. *Webster's Home University Dictionary, 1958*

Cacao is, most simply, where chocolate begins. It is the pods of the cacao tree that produce the seeds we grind down into chocolate. Cacao trees only grow and flourish in rain-forest conditions 5 degrees above or below the equator, making countries like Mexico, Venezuela, Colombia, Madagascar, the Ivory Coast, and the West Indies prime chocolate growers. The cacao pod falls from the tree when ripe and literally rots on the rain-forest floor. The seeds then ferment, becoming perfect for grinding down into cocoa and cocoa butter. These two elements are separated during processing, only to be brought back together again with milk solids and sugar to make your favorite chocolate treat.

The amount of cacao present in the chocolate we consume determines how dark and bitter it is. A milk chocolate bar may contain anywhere from 10% to 40% cacao. A bittersweet or dark chocolate bar generally contains 60% cacao. You can find chocolate bars on the market as dark as 99% cacao. These bars contain only cacao and cocoa butter, making them very bitter—not the type of chocolate to satisfy a sweet tooth!

White chocolate contains no cacao and so is not truly chocolate. This makes white chocolate a misnomer (we love saying that!). These bars are made from cocoa butter, sugar, and milk solids only.

Begin the tasting with the most basic, darkest chocolate you have. Continue passing the chocolates in order from dark to light to white (from bitter to sweet). Explain the cacao percentage in each, which is always printed on packages of high-quality chocolate. If it is not, the basic rules are, dark is 60% cacao, milk is 30% to 40%, and white is 0%. (For more info on cacao, see sidebar.)

A fun twist is to mix things up. Do the tasting with both high-quality chocolates and mass-produced chocolates, but keep all chocolate brand labels out of sight. Can your guests tell the cheap stuff from the chic stuff?

Everybody has an opinion, so let's hear it. After each tasting ask the guest to describe each chocolate. Be forewarned: This is where you may hear the phrase "earthy undertones." We usually use a number system to keep the overused adjectives to a minimum (1 is fantastic, 5 is horrific).

After one round of passing, fill up the glasses, turn up the tunes, and put out any extra chocolate if you have any. Dinner is not necessary at this point.

swank recipes

chocolate hennessey fondue

YIELD: 4 SERVINGS

Fondue is like a fashion trend: forever going in and out of style. Once synonymous with seventies clichés (bell-bottoms, polyester, and disco), fondue is back in vogue again. This version is an homage to that beloved decade—a study in chocolate, liquor, and groovy dipping accompaniments.

Fondue:

7 ounces good-quality dark chocolate (such as E. Guittard), chopped
3 ounces good-quality milk chocolate (such as E. Guittard), chopped
¾ cup heavy cream
1 tablespoon unsalted butter, softened to room temperature
1 to 2 tablespoons Hennessey VSOP

Accompaniments:

Fresh fruit and berries
Large fresh mint leaves, cleaned and dried (wonderful to dip)
Pound cake, cut into cubes
Biscotti
Homemade Marshmallows (recipe follows)
Cinnamon Pastry Straws (recipe follows)

Homemade Marshmallows:

2 tablespoons gelatin powder (3 packets)
1 cup cold water
1⅓ cups granulated sugar
½ cup corn syrup
Pinch of salt
4 teaspoons vanilla paste (see page 188 for where to buy), or 2 teaspoons vanilla extract
1 tablespoon unsalted butter
1 cup confectioners' sugar, sifted, for dusting

Cinnamon Pastry Straws:

¼ cup Demerara or turbinado sugar (available at most health food stores)
¼ teaspoon ground cinnamon
1 sheet frozen puff pastry, thawed

Prepare the fondue:

Combine the dark and milk chocolates in a large mixing bowl. Pour the cream into a small, heavy-bottomed pot and place over medium heat. Heat the cream until hot to the touch but not boiling. (You do not want to scorch the milk.) Beadlike bubbles will form around the edge of the pan. Pour the hot cream over the chocolate and gently whisk until the chocolate is melted. Add the butter and whisk until smooth. Pour in the Hennessey and mix until smooth. (If you want to thin out your fondue, add 2 tablespoons.) Transfer the mixture to your favorite fondue pot and keep warm.

Prepare the marshmallows:

Grease the bottom and sides of an 8 x 12 x 3-inch pan and generously dust with approximately ¼ cup confectioners' sugar.

In a standing mixer fitted with the whip attachment, sprinkle the gelatin over ⅔ cup cold water and let stand for 15 minutes.

Boil the granulated sugar, corn syrup, ⅓ cup water, and salt in a heavy 3-quart saucepan until an instant-read thermometer registers 250° F.

With your mixer set on moderately low speed, carefully pour the sugar mixture toward the side of the bowl. Increase the mixer speed to moderately high and whip until the mixture has increased sixfold in volume and holds stiff peaks. Add the vanilla paste or extract until combined.

Transfer the mixture to the prepared pan using a buttered rubber spatula or scraper. Smooth out the top and dust generously with ¼ cup confectioners' sugar. Let sit overnight, uncovered.

Remove from the pan, dust sharp scissors with confectioners' sugar, and cut the marshmallow mixture into 1-inch squares. Coat with the remaining ½ cup of confectioners' sugar. Keep in airtight sealable bags.

Prepare the cinnamon pastry straws:

Preheat the oven to 400° F. Line two baking sheets with parchment paper.

Whisk together the sugar and cinnamon in a shallow bowl.

Carefully lay out the chilled puff pastry on a large cutting board. If there are any damp areas, blot them dry with a paper towel. Sprinkle generously with cinnamon-sugar to cover and in one quick motion, turn over to the other side. Gently rub in the remaining cinnamon-sugar to cover, and using a large, sharp knife, cut the puff pastry into ½-inch-wide strips along the short end. Twist the ends of each strip of puff pastry in opposite directions into spiral straws. Repeat with the remaining strips. Transfer to baking sheets and bake for 12 to 15 minutes, until golden brown.

Cool to room temperature and keep in an airtight container. Will keep for two days.

s'mores tart

YIELD: ONE 11-INCH TART

We turned the campfire classic into a classic tart. It's less messy in this form, but every bit as rich, gooey, and intense. Feel free to substitute the Homemade Marshmallows on page 118 for the Minty Marshmallows.

Minty Marshmallows:

1 tablespoon unsalted butter
3 packets gelatin powder
1 cup cold water
1⅓ cups sugar
1 cup packed fresh mint
⅓ cup water
½ cup corn syrup
Pinch salt
1 cup confectioners' sugar, sifted

Great Graham Tart Crust:

1 cup all-purpose flour
¼ cup whole wheat flour
2 tablespoons granulated sugar
3 tablespoons light brown sugar
½ teaspoon ground cinnamon
½ teaspoon baking powder
¼ teaspoon baking soda
½ teaspoon salt
2 tablespoons unsalted butter
2 tablespoons shortening
2 tablespoons honey
1 tablespoon molasses
1 teaspoon vanilla extract

2 tablespoons cold water

1 tablespoon turbinado sugar

Chocolate Cream:

10 ounces semisweet chocolate, finely chopped

1½ cups heavy cream

¼ cup Grand Marnier

1 tablespoon unsalted butter, softened

Prepare the marshmallows:

Grease the bottom and sides of an 8 x 13 x 3-inch pan with butter and generously dust with approximately ¼ cup confectioners' sugar.

In a standing mixer fitted with the whip attachment, sprinkle the gelatin over ⅔ cup cold water and let stand for 15 minutes.

In a heavy 3-quart saucepan, bring the sugar, ⅓ cup water, and mint to a boil. Remove from the heat, cover with a tight-fitting lid, and steep for 30 minutes. Pour the mixture through a sieve, pressing on the mint with the back of a spoon, and discard the remaining solids. Return the liquid to the pan and add the corn syrup and salt. Boil until an instant-read thermometer registers 250° F.

Set your mixer on moderately low speed and carefully pour the sugar toward the sides of the bowl. Increase the mixer speed to moderately high and whip until the mixture has increased six times in volume and holds stiff peaks.

Transfer the mixture to the prepared pan using a buttered rubber spatula or scraper. Smooth out the top and dust generously with ¼ cup confectioners' sugar. Let sit overnight, uncovered.

Remove from the pan, dust sharp scissors with confectioners' sugar, and cut the marshmallow mixture into 1-inch squares. Coat with the remaining confectioners' sugar. Keep in airtight sealable bags.

Prepare the crust:

Preheat the oven to 350° F and place racks in the upper and lower positions. Lightly butter an 11-inch fluted tart pan with a removable bottom.

In a standing mixer fitted with the paddle attachment, mix all of the dry ingredients. Add the butter and shortening and mix on low speed until sandy and coarse. Add the honey, molasses, and vanilla and mix until the mixture is sandy. Add the cold water and mix. If the mixture looks dry, add a teaspoon of water at a time just until the dough holds together and comes away from the sides of the bowl. Wrap the dough in plastic wrap and chill for 1 hour, until firm.

On a well-floured surface, roll the dough to less than ¼ inch thick and press into the tart pan.

Bake for 20 to 25 minutes, until golden, and cool to room temperature.

Prepare the chocolate cream:

Place the chocolate in a large bowl. Boil the cream in a heavy 1-quart saucepan and pour over the chocolate. Use a whisk to stir gently until the chocolate is melted and the mixture is smooth. Add the Grand Marnier and mix in the butter.

Pour into the baked tart shell and smooth the top. Allow to cool to room temperature, approximately 30 minutes, then chill until firm, 4 hours or overnight.

To assemble the tart:

Preheat the broiler. Cover the tart with marshmallows and place it 4 to 6 inches from the broiler for 1 to 2 minutes, until the marshmallows begin to brown and blister. Be sure to keep the oven door slightly ajar and watch carefully that the topping does not burn. Cool to room temperature and cut into sixteen very thin slices.

marshmallow and chocolate: a love story

Like peanut butter, the marshmallow is an important part of the chocolate diet. It is almost a necessity in hot chocolate and fondue, and it is famed and celebrated for its starring role in the S'more.

Anecdotal evidence suggests that the original marshmallow was initially created as a medicinal candy to soothe sore throats. Doctors would extract the sap of a marshmallow plant—a real plant indigenous to salt marshes and bogs—and blend it with egg whites and sugar into a hardened cough-drop-like confection. Over time, the sap was replaced with gelatin and corn syrup, and the purported "healing" properties of the marshmallow were annulled.

The marshmallow went through many interpretations in the early part of the 1900's, alternately puffy, gooey, extra sweet, and remarkably dry before eventually leaving its indelible mark in the form of the puffy, dry marshmallow known for making the perfect S'more. Fashioned by those wild and wacky gals, The Girl Scouts, the classic S'more recipe was first published in *Tramping and Trailing with Girl Scouts of the USA* in 1927.

Today the marshmallow is making a gourmet comeback. It is appearing in top restaurants all gussied up as a melt-in-your-mouth dream often infused with lemon or mint and topped with chocolate and/or coconut.

We advise you to make your own; they are well worth the effort.

spiced cocoa meatballs

YIELD: 12 MEATBALLS

These meatballs have a spicy flavor with strong hints of cinnamon as well as ginger. The unsweetened cocoa powder and fresh mint give complementary undertones that round out the flavor, while the ancho chile provides smokiness rather than heat in the sauce.

Meatballs:

½ cup coarse dried bread crumbs
¼ cup milk
1 pound ground beef
½ cup finely minced onion
1 tablespoon finely minced fresh garlic
½ teaspoon ground cinnamon
½ teaspoon unsweetened cocoa powder
½ teaspoon ground ginger
1 teaspoon minced fresh mint leaves
1 teaspoon light brown sugar
2 tablespoons oil

Sauce:

1 tablespoon vegetable oil
1 ancho chile
2 tablespoons tomato paste
1 bay leaf
½ cup red wine
1 cup water or chicken stock
½ teaspoon salt
¼ teaspoon black pepper
1 tablespoon Wondra flour

Prepare the meatballs:

Soak the bread crumbs in the milk until softened, about 5 minutes. Mix together with the remaining meatball ingredients except the oil and refrigerate for 1 hour, until chilled. Shape into twelve 2-inch balls.

Heat the 2 tablespoons of oil in a nonstick skillet over moderately high heat. Add the meatballs, leaving a 1-inch space in between. Gently stir until the meatballs are browned on all sides. Remove and transfer to drain on paper towels.

Prepare the sauce:

Heat the tablespoon of oil in a heavy 3-quart saucepan over moderate heat. Stirring constantly, add the chile, tomato paste, and bay leaf and cook until fragrant. Add the red wine and simmer for about 2 minutes. Add the water or chicken stock and simmer for 3 minutes. Pour the sauce through a sieve and discard the solids. Return to the saucepan and season with salt and pepper. Whisk in the flour over moderate heat until thickened. Add the meatballs and gently stir to coat. Cover and simmer for 20 minutes. Serve in small dishes with sauce and garnish with chopped mint if desired.

Notes: You can vary the size of the meatballs, making them larger or smaller. The recipe quantities can easily be doubled for larger parties. Note that the amount of sauce is minimal, as the meatballs are the star of this dish, so if you want more sauce, simply double the sauce recipe. This recipe also freezes well.

on the savory side

Bittersweet chocolate and cocoa are perfect ingredients to incorporate into your savory recipes. They have appeared to great acclaim in soups, chilies, salad dressings, and spice rubs.

When attempting to work chocolate into some of your traditional savory courses, we offer a few pointers:

- Use only good quality bittersweet chocolate. Experiment with percentages between 60% and 84%.
- Start by adding very small amounts. The desired effect is to enhance the original flavors, not to overpower them.
- We'd like to think that chocolate works well with any savory dish, but we must be honest, there are some food items that simply shouldn't be paired with this ingredient. Don't despair if your savory chocolate experiment fails—just move on to the next one.

Need a quick and savory chocolate appetizer? We particularly love the blessed pairing of bittersweet chocolate and coarse salt in this easy recipe.

chocolate toast

Slice a fresh baguette into approximately 1-inch slices and place on cookie sheet, flat side down. Turn your oven to broil and place the cookie sheet in the middle rack until the slices just begin to brown. Remove from the oven and brush slices with olive oil. Top each slice with a few bittersweet chocolate curls or small chips. Return to the oven for about 1 minute or until chocolate has just started to melt. Remove the sheet from the oven and sprinkle slices with a coarse fleur de sel or sea salt. Serve to your guests immediately.

mole skewers

YIELD: 3½ CUPS SAUCE TO COVER ABOUT 6 DOZEN SMALL BAMBOO SKEWERS

Mole is typically thought of as a savory Mexican sauce with chilies and chocolate but actually appears in many different varieties, sometimes without chocolate. Don't be afraid of the long list of ingredients; the results are well worth it. The classic rendition of mole is usually in the form of a stew, but here, mole acts instead as a sauce. It's great on the grill or used for basting—and of course it has chocolate.

Note that mole is requisite party food on any notable chocolate occasion and easily converts to a vegetarian version. Small skewers are great handheld party food, but this recipe works just as well (and faster) with larger-sized skewers for a larger portion, to be plated. This recipe makes a generous batch of sauce and is best made a day or two ahead to allow the flavors to develop. The chocolate used in this recipe is a special type of sweet Mexican chocolate with cinnamon, also called Ibarra or Abuelita (available in ethnic and specialty markets).

2 dried mulatto chilies (about 1 ounce)
2 dried ancho chilies (about 1 ounce)
2 dried pasilla chilies (about 1 ounce)
2 tablespoons sesame seeds
1 tablespoon vegetable oil
2 cloves fresh garlic, peeled
1 small onion, peeled and sliced ½ inch thick
1 tablespoon raisins
⅛ cup whole almonds with skins
One 14-ounce can peeled whole tomatoes
¼ teaspoon ground cinnamon
¼ teaspoon dried oregano (preferably Mexican)
¼ teaspoon black pepper

Pinch ground cloves

½ (3.3-ounce) tablet Mexican chocolate (such as Ibarra or Abuelita), chopped fine

1 slice firm white sandwich bread, toasted dark brown and coarsely chopped

One 14-ounce can chicken broth plus 1 empty can filled with water, or 3½ cups water

1 teaspoon salt

2 pounds skinless boneless chicken breast, pork loin, or firm tofu cut into 1-inch cubes

2 pounds zucchini, quartered lengthwise and cut into 1-inch pieces

2 pounds small boiling onions, outer skin, root, and top ends removed, cut into halves (about 1½ inches in diameter)

Vegetable oil for greasing

Heat a dry 12-inch nonstick heavy skillet over moderately high heat and toast the chilies, pressing down on all sides. (The chilies will puff, making it easier to expose more surface area as they pucker and the skins change color slightly.) Remove from the skillet and place on a cutting board. Remove and discard the stems, then cut down the side and remove and discard the seeds. Rinse the chilies in cold water, then soak them in a large bowl of boiling-hot water for 30 minutes. Drain the chilies and chop fine. Transfer to a blender and add 1 cup of chicken broth or water. Mix on low speed to make a paste. Heat a 12-inch nonstick heavy skillet over moderate heat and add the chili paste. Cook, stirring constantly, until the mixture is thick like tomato paste, about 5 to 10 minutes. Remove from the heat and transfer to a bowl.

Heat a dry 12-inch nonstick heavy skillet over moderate heat and add the sesame seeds. Stir constantly until golden brown, about 3 to 5 minutes. Remove from the pan and return the skillet to the stove over moderate heat until hot but not smoking. Add 1 tablespoon of oil to coat. Add the garlic, onion, and almonds and sauté until the onions are softened and the almonds turn golden, about 5 minutes. Transfer the mixture to a bowl with the chili paste using a slotted spoon and reserve any remaining oil in skillet.

Add the raisins to the skillet and cook, stirring constantly until puffed and slightly browned, about 1 to 2 minutes. Add 1½ tablespoons of the toasted sesame seeds (reserve the remainder for garnish), tomatoes with juice, chili paste, onion mixture, cinnamon, oregano, black pepper, cloves, and chocolate, and bring to a gentle simmer until the chocolate is melted. Remove from the heat and transfer the mixture to a blender. Add the bread and pulse until the mixture is just combined, then add the remaining chicken broth or 1 cup of water and blend until smooth.

Pour the mixture through a mesh strainer into a heavy 4- to 6-quart pot, pushing down on the solids with the back of a ladle. Discard the solids. Stir in 1½ cups water. Return to a boil and simmer, stirring occasionally, over moderately low heat until mixture is reduced by half, about 45 minutes. Skim off and discard any foam or oil. Stir in salt to taste and remove from the heat. Let cool to room temperature. If not using immediately, keep covered and chilled (see Note).

Season the chicken, pork, or tofu with salt and pepper, then transfer to a large mixing bowl. (Season the tofu in one layer.)

Submerge (3½-inch) bamboo skewers in water. (This makes it easier to skewer the meat.)

Preheat the oven to 400° F. Set oven racks in upper and lower positions. Brush two large baking sheets with oil.

Reserve 1 cup of mole sauce for basting and generously coat the meat or tofu and vegetables separately with the remaining sauce. Spear the skewers with any combination of meat and vegetables you prefer.

Bring the remaining mole sauce to a boil in a heavy 1-quart saucepan and keep it warm.

Arrange the skewers ½ inch apart on the baking sheets. Place the trays in the upper and lower thirds of the oven for 5 minutes, then remove from the oven and generously baste the skewers with the remaining sauce.

Return the trays to the oven, switching top and bottom baking positions, and bake until the meat is just cooked through, 5 to 10 minutes more.

Sprinkle the skewers with the remaining sesame seeds. Serve warm or at room temperature.

Notes: You may make the mole sauce one week ahead, if you wish, or make larger quantities and keep frozen in an airtight container for up to three months. Place the reserved mole sauce in ramekins, gravy boats, or regular cups and place at the dinner table for your guests who want extra.

Do you want Extra Spicy Mole? Double the amount of chilies in the recipe for some extra fire and smoke.

chasing the mole

We tasted an authentic mole in a tiny town on the outskirts of Cozumel and, like any culinary revelation, it was an immediate and life-changing moment. The mole negro was thick, earthy, and complex, as opposed to the runny, simplified chocolate chili liquid that had been our previous barometer of mole success. Now that we had experienced this taste sensation, there was no turning back.

Our search for the perfect stateside mole has never ended. Unfortunately, this search has been hampered and complicated by a number of factors. First, the term "mole" is eclectic and variable. According to Zarela Martinez in *The Food and Life of Oaxaca,* a mole has no exact and definable ingredients. They are usually based on "ground dried chilies sometimes in elaborate combinations of varieties".

Secondly, moles tend to have *a lot* of ingredients and require a large amount of elaborate pre-preparation. In essence, not a high profit item for a restaurant's bottom line.

Finally, more traditional moles contain lard, which is an alarming ingredient for many people.

Throughout the years, we have noticed the variety and the taste of Americanized moles have improved greatly. Previously hard-to-find fresh ingredients are more readily available, and there appears to be a renewed interest in serious Mexican cuisine.

For the home cook, we wish them the best of luck. Preparing a homemade mole is a bit of a task, but well worth the effort. For those not in the mood to cook, perhaps it is time to book that trip to Mexico that you have been dreaming about.

white chocolate lemon cream mousse

YIELD: EIGHT ½-CUP SERVINGS

We are equal-opportunity chocolate purveyors, and we wanted to give white chocolate its due in this recipe. This is a pure and intense burst of white chocolate balanced with a hint of lemon, but be forewarned: This dessert is definitely on the sweeter side.

12 ounces good-quality white chocolate, chopped into small pieces (not chips)
1¼ cups heavy cream
4 large egg yolks
1 teaspoon finely grated lemon zest
¼ cup fresh lemon juice
¼ cup sugar

Place the chocolate in a clean, dry, large mixing bowl over a pan of simmering water, making sure the bottom of the bowl does not touch the water. Melt the chocolate over low heat, stirring occasionally, and add ¼ cup of the cream. Mix to combine. The mixture may become stiff or separate but will loosen up and become smooth.

While the chocolate is melting, whip the remaining 1 cup of cream until soft peaks form; keep refrigerated.

In a standing mixer fitted with the whip attachment, mix the yolks on high speed until pale and fluffy, about 3 minutes.

While the yolks are mixing, boil the lemon zest, juice, and sugar in a 1-quart saucepan until large bubbles form and an instant-read thermometer registers 250° F. (You may have to tip the pan carefully to get an accurate reading.)

Reduce the mixer speed to moderately low and carefully pour the lemon mixture gradually toward the sides of the bowl. Increase the mixer speed to moderately high and whip until the exterior of the bowl is just slightly warmer than your hands—about 2 to 3 minutes.

Remove the bowl and whip from the mixer. Some zest may stick to the whip; if so, simply scrape it back into the bowl. Using a spatula, fold in the melted white chocolate until well combined. Gently fold in one-third of the whipped cream until mixed, then fold in the remaining cream until just combined. Do not overmix.

Transfer the mixture to small serving glasses or dishes or one large serving dish. Chill, covered with plastic wrap, until set, about 4 hours or overnight.

This mousse won't be very viscous at first, but it sets up as it chills. Use it as a layer in cakes or as a plated dessert.

To make simple quenelles (oval shapes), warm a large spoon under hot water, dry it, then scoop along the surface of the mousse to shape small mounds. Transfer to a dessert plate and serve with fresh berries and different sauces. Garnish with white chocolate shavings and finely grated lemon zest.

shiny chocolate-orange tartlettes

YIELD: 8 TARTLETTES

There are three different components in these fabulous little gems—tart shells, rich filling, and homemade marmalade.

The recipe for this easy marmalade makes more than you'll need for the tartlette, but it's so good, you'll want extra for your morning toast.

The tart dough is light, flaky, and great-tasting on its own. This dough can be made in larger quantities and is great for full-size tarts too (adjust the baking time).

The chocolate-orange filling here is simply decadent and just sinful enough for eight lucky people. It's important to let the filling set properly. If the shine is somehow lost, simply warm it in a hot oven for a few seconds, until the top becomes shiny again.

Orange-Vanilla Marmalade:

2 navel oranges, whole and unpeeled
1½ cups sugar
½ vanilla bean, split and scraped
¼ cup fresh orange juice

Dough:

2 cups all-purpose flour
1 teaspoon grated orange zest
¼ cup sugar
Pinch salt
1½ sticks (6 ounces) unsalted butter, cut into small bits and softened
About 2 tablespoons cold water

Filling:

12 ounces good-quality semisweet chocolate, chopped

1 cup heavy cream

2 tablespoons Orange-Vanilla Marmalade

2 tablespoons unsalted butter, softened

Prepare the marmalade:

Place oranges in a deep bowl and cover them with boiling-hot water. Let them stand for 5 minutes, then rinse them in cold water and repeat. Rinse again. Cut off and discard the ends, then cut them in half and cut out the center cores, removing any tough membranes or pits. Slice each orange half into ¼-inch slices and chop fine. Transfer to a heavy 1-quart saucepan and add the sugar, vanilla bean, and orange juice. Simmer over low heat, stirring occasionally until the liquid is reduced and the mixture has thickened, about 1 hour. Remove from the heat and transfer to a heatproof bowl. Cool to room temperature. Cover and keep refrigerated for up to 2 weeks, or seal in sterilized jars. Leave the vanilla bean in the marmalade to keep the flavoring, but do not eat it.

Prepare the dough:

Place an oven rack in the middle position and preheat the oven to 375° F.

In a large bowl, whisk together the flour, zest, sugar, and salt. Using your hands or a pastry blender, cut in the butter until small pea-sized lumps form and the mixture looks sandy. Add water, 1 tablespoon at a time, and gently mix until the dough just comes together. Press the dough into two balls. Place each ball between two large sheets of plastic wrap and roll out into a ¼-inch-thick square. Refrigerate until firm, about 1 hour.

Remove one portion of dough and roll it out slightly to even it out and soften it slightly. Arrange four 4 x ¾-inch nonstick tart molds touching each other (like a square) on a work surface. Remove one layer of plastic wrap from one-half of the dough and place the dough directly on the tart molds (the plastic side should be on top). Remove the plastic and press the dough into each tart shell using the back of an espresso spoon. Fill any cracks or holes with excess dough.

Repeat with the remaining dough to make eight tartlettes. Lightly prick the bottom of each tartlette with a fork and place on a sheet pan.

Lightly butter eight small pieces of aluminum foil and line them against the dough to cover the interior of each tart. Fill with pie weights or baking beans and bake for 20 to 25 minutes, until the edges appear golden. Remove the tarts from the oven, carefully remove the foil and pie weights, then return to the oven to bake until the tart shells are golden, 3 to 5 minutes more. Remove from the oven and cool on a wire rack. Unmold the tart shells when cool. These tarts can be made ahead and kept in an airtight container for three days.

Prepare the filling:

Place the chocolate in a large mixing bowl. Bring the cream and marmalade to a boil in a heavy 1-quart saucepan. Remove from the heat and pour over the chocolate, stirring gently with a whisk until smooth. Do not beat or incorporate air. Add the butter and continue to stir with a whisk until smooth. Assemble the tarts immediately, filling each baked tart shell three-quarters full. Set in the refrigerator if the room is warm, or let sit in a cool room undisturbed for 1 hour. (This helps keep the shine—a humid refrigerator can dull the surface.)

Garnish the tartlettes with a small dollop of orange marmalade, if desired, and sprinkle raw or sanding sugar on top. Add chocolate shavings if desired.

versatile hot chocolate

YIELD: 2 TO 3 SERVINGS

We have several nicknames for this favorite drink of ours: Liquid Candy Bar, Melted Chocolate, Party Pick-Me-Up in a Cup. Call it what you will, just promise us you will never again use those little supermarket-brand envelopes of powdered pseudo-hot chocolate. Our recipe is rich without being overwhelming, and it works well with almost any addition.

3 ounces bittersweet (60% to 70%) chocolate, chopped into small pieces
¼ cup water
¼ cup heavy cream
½ cup milk
2 teaspoons light brown sugar

Place chopped chocolate in a small heatproof bowl. Bring water to boil and pour over chocolate pieces, making sure all the chocolate pieces are submerged. Set aside for about 3 minutes. While waiting for chocolate to melt, place cream and milk in a medium saucepan and bring mixture to a simmer. Stir in brown sugar.

Whisk chocolate and water mixture until smooth, then pour immediately into milk and cream mixture. Whisking constantly, bring mixture just to a boil. Divide the hot chocolate among the mugs and serve immediately.

Variations:

Spiked Hot Chocolate

Add a shot of liquor to your mug of hot chocolate. Peppermint schnapps, Kahlua, and any orange-flavored liquors work well. Only add the shot to the mug after you have prepared your hot chocolate, never during the cooking process.

Iced Hot Chocolate

Hot chocolate tastes great chilled. Bring your hot chocolate to room temperature while it is still in the saucepan. Once it's cooled, fill an ice-cube tray with some of the hot chocolate and place the rest in a pitcher in the refrigerator. After the ice cubes are completely frozen, place three or four in a glass. Shake your pitcher of iced hot chocolate (some chocolate will settle at the bottom of the pitcher), and pour over the ice cubes.

chocolate martini

YIELD: 1 SERVING

A chocolate martini is not a serious drink. It is strictly a fun concoction, specially blended for parties and light-hearted socializing. Our recipe is easy enough for the home mixologist and swank enough for the discerning martini drinker.

½ tablespoon good-quality Dutch process cocoa powder
½ tablespoon sugar
1½ shots chocolate liqueur
1½ shots crème de cacao
½ shot vanilla-flavored vodka
2½ shots half-and-half

Mix cocoa and sugar together. Rim a chilled martini class with water and dip into cocoa-and-sugar mixture. Shake chocolate liqueur, Crème de Cacao, vodka, and half-and-half in a cocktail shaker over ice. Pour into martini glass.

the "shaker"

YIELD: 1 SERVING

This is Chocolate Bar's most popular summer drink. A "shaker" is really just a twist on your typical chocolate-coffee drink. The shaking action creates a perfect frothy, foamy head for the mixture. Sprinkle with cocoa or top with a dab of chocolate syrup (page 82) for a decadent display.

1 shot fresh espresso
8 ounces chilled iced chocolate (page 138)
Handful ice
Whipped cream (optional)

Place the espresso, iced chocolate, and ice in a cocktail shaker and shake over ice. Strain the ingredients into a chilled cocktail glass. Top with whipped cream if desired.

Variations:

Chocolate-Orange Shaker

Add a tablespoon of Grand Marnier to the cocktail-shaker ingredients.

Mint-Chip Shaker

Add a tablespoon of peppermint syrup to the cocktail-shaker ingredients.

the future is now

Chocolate is in a constant state of evolution.

The shape, taste, consistency, and utility of chocolate are broadening and expanding at a rapid pace. While chocolate has always been popular, its status is beyond mere confection. Chocolate is art. Chocolate is fashion. Chocolate is architecture. Chocolate is a movie star—think *Chocolat* and *Like Water for Chocolate*! On principle, we like our chocolate to be unadorned, simple, and bold without any unnecessary modifications. On occasion, however, we do feel the pull of an inspired chocolate sculpture or an artistically rendered cocoa-butter painting.

While artists are welcome to work with chocolate, we prefer to eat it.

CHOCOLATE BY DESIGN

The Shape of Things

As long as there is chocolate, there will be people to shape and mold it, for better and for worse. The clichés of molded chocolate will assault you: chocolate Easter bunnies; chocolate hearts; chocolate pumpkins; Statue of Liberty chocolates; Eiffel Tower chocolates; Las Vegas chocolate dice; sexy anatomy chocolates (these are particularly inappropriate and oftentimes hideous); and endless variations on corporate logos in chocolate and mascots as chocolates. The clichés can be forgiven and even understandable as long as the chocolate tastes extraordinary. Unfortunately, there is an expectation that poor-quality chocolate will be excused if it comes in a delightful (or dreadful) mold. Never excuse bad chocolate! We don't care what it looks like.

Thankfully, there are a few master chocolate sculptors turning chocolate into true art. These chocolate visionaries are just as influenced by modern architecture, furniture design, and sculpture as they are by Monet, Picasso, and Rembrandt. Who and what influences you? Whether it's Matisse or *Mad Magazine*, we encourage you to apply your own artistic license to create your vision in chocolate.

Guittard

The Color Is in the Butter

Within one week of opening Chocolate Bar, we noticed a trend. Chocolate bonbons decorated with colors and swirls and images clearly outsold the plainer ones—flavor was rarely a deciding factor. As members of a very visual society, one that adores a bit of flair mixed with the unusual and cleverly designed, this should not have come as a surprise to us. We spend hours painstakingly decorating our homes, setting our holiday dinner tables, pursuing the newest trends in fashion, design, architecture, and even gardening. Why shouldn't our bonbons be just as cutting edge, gorgeous, and intricate?

The colored designs found on top of bonbons are cocoa-butter transfers. Film-transfer sheets are printed with vegetable-colored cocoa butter. A sheet is laid on top of the chocolate before it sets. Once set, the sheet is pulled off, leaving the dyed cocoa-butter design behind.

Although the transfer sheet is the most popular method of adding cocoa-butter designs to bonbons (you can make hundreds at a time), some chocolatiers paint designs directly onto chocolate bars the same way artists paint canvases. We have seen pictures of people, replicas of paintings, and logo designs painted onto large chocolate bars, bonbons, and ganache-iced cakes. You can even paint cocoa butter into a mold before pouring in the chocolate and create a colorful chocolate egg or painted pumpkin as a result. There are no limits when using cocoa butter; we only ask that you make sure to use high-quality chocolate. Again, it doesn't matter how pretty it is if it doesn't taste good!

stuff for your molding and sculpting toolbox

There are plenty of places to purchase traditional candy and chocolate molds (see page 177 for sources) for the essential holiday shapes. Order your pumpkin shapes, your snowmen molds, and your valentine hearts from these trusted sources, but don't be afraid to be a pioneer. Search out the unusual, create something unique—explore your molding, shaping, and sculpting options:

- Think about using soap molds for your chocolate creations. They usually come in larger and more geometrical shapes than traditional chocolate molds.

- Pour tempered chocolate into ordinary ice-cube trays to create mini chocolate bars.

- Give your molded chocolate some texture—press leaves, blades of grass, flowers, bubble wrap, and any other clean, unusual object onto your chocolate.

- Don't be afraid to use real tools. Think paintbrushes and putty knives (as long as they're clean!), both of which can add texture to your chocolate creations.

- A pair of tweezers is perfect for placing or removing delicate flowers, transfers, or other small items.

CHOCOLATE: IT'S NOT JUST FOR EATING ANYMORE

Chocolate is broadening in spectrum and appeal at a very rapid pace. No longer confined to chocolate desserts, it is popping up in some expected and unexpected places.

Serious Brew

When the temperature drops and the thirst for a chocolate drink kicks in, think past hot cocoa and consider a hearty dark beer. Chocolate is making seasonal appearances in a few select mass-produced stouts, often available only in the winter. The idea is to evoke the taste and feeling of a malted chocolate drink with a hint of bourbon. Stouts make a perfect accompaniment to most chocolate desserts.

The Sweet Smell of Chocolate

Want to entice your love? How about smelling like a freshly baked brownie? Warm chocolate-scented fragrances are available to set the mood. Would you like to have the delicious aroma of hot cocoa wafting through your kitchen, without ever touching an ingredient? Simply light a candle or spritz some room spray. Some companies offer atomizers to scent your home in heady fragrances, including chocolate-chip cookie and chocolate cake. You can even pour yourself a bubble bath simmering with the essence of cocoa. Chocolate as aromatherapy is pleasant and light, though it does makes us hunger for the real thing.

Bodylicious

Beauty companies are creating lines inspired by, and in some instances containing, chocolate and cocoa. Some brands tout the pleasurable aspects of chocolate with edible body powder (who needs to order dessert when you're wearing it?) and lickable lip gloss (perfect for snacking *and* moisturizing!).

Other beauty products and world-class spas actually boast of the "ben-

efits" of chocolate and its derivatives: cocoa powder as exfoliant, cocoa butter as moisturizer, chocolate as a natural color. Who knew? Cocoa butter has long been a mainstay at drugstores nationwide. It's touted as the cure-all for every skin problem, from scars to stretch marks. Whether or not the claims are true, cocoa butter remains one of the most popular moisturizers on the market.

Chocolate Fashion

Chocolate fashion has now made its way into a boutique near you, and couture designers are realizing that chocolate is *always* in fashion, no matter the season. We've seen purses, dresses, and skirts printed and embroidered with images of chocolate bars and truffles. Some designers sell their own brands of chocolate bars in their boutiques! People are even wearing skirts and shirts and dresses *made out of chocolate* (if only for a very short time), as witnessed at the annual Chocolate Shows in Paris and New York.

We, too, are guilty of using chocolate as fashion statement and we apologize, but it was too hard to resist. Our "Chocolate Boy" and "Chocolate Girl" T-shirts are top-selling items in our store and online.

The saying "people can't get enough of the stuff" holds true. Whether it's flavored by or inspired by—chocolate's not just for eating anymore.

artistic recipes

the ultimate sauces

These are a few of the ultimate sauces for your ultimate desserts. Use them to enhance your pound cakes, cakes, ice creams, fruits, marshmallows, cookies, biscotti, and any variety of accompaniments. There are no right or wrong combinations, so feel free to experiment.

Chocolate-Jasmine Sauce

YIELD: 1½ CUPS

6 ounces bittersweet chocolate, chopped fine
1 cup half-and-half
3 tablespoons sugar
¼ cup good-quality jasmine tea leaves (see Note)

Place the chocolate in a bowl. In a saucepan, whisk the half-and-half with the sugar over moderate heat until dissolved and bring to a boil. Remove from the heat and whisk in the tea leaves. Cover and steep for 10 minutes. Return the mixture to a boil and pour through a fine-mesh strainer into the bowl with the chocolate. Gently whisk to combine and cool to room temperature or serve warm.

Note: Chocolate Peppermint Patty Tea from the Chocolate Bar also works very nicely in this recipe.

Classic Raspberry Coulis

YIELD: 1 CUP

12 ounces frozen or fresh raspberries
½ cup confectioners' sugar
¼ cup water
1 teaspoon fresh lemon juice

Combine all of the ingredients in a heavy 1-quart saucepan and bring to a boil. Puree in a food processor or with a hand blender and pour through a strainer. Cool and season to taste with lemon juice. Will keep refrigerated for 1 week.

Chocolate-Espresso Sauce

YIELD: 2 CUPS

6 ounces bittersweet chocolate, chopped fine
½ cup milk
¾ cup heavy cream
½ cup sugar
½ cup strong brewed espresso coffee

Place the chocolate in a large heatproof bowl. Whisk the milk, cream, and sugar in a 1-quart saucepan over high heat. Bring to a boil and remove from the heat. Pour over the chocolate and add the espresso. Whisk gently until smooth and combined.

Chocolate Bar Cool-Aid Sauce

YIELD: 1 CUP

½ cup Chocolate Bar Cool-Aid Tea leaves (see Note)
1½ cups very hot water
3 tablespoons acacia honey
2 teaspoons cornstarch

Place the tea in a large bowl and pour hot water over it. Cover and steep for 20 minutes. Pour through a fine-mesh sieve into a heavy 1-quart saucepan. Add the honey and whisk together over moderately high heat.

Place the cornstarch in a small bowl. Add ¼ cup of tea to the bowl and mix well until the cornstarch has dissolved. Whisk the cornstarch mixture into the saucepan and until smooth. Bring to a boil, whisking constantly, and pour through a fine mesh sieve. Allow to cool.

Note: Cool-Aid Tea is a blend of hibiscus and blood orange tea available from the Chocolate Bar. If unavailable, use a rose-hip-and-hibiscus-berry tea.

Minted Chocolate Sauce

YIELD: 2 CUPS

10 ounces bittersweet chocolate, chopped
1 cup milk
½ cup heavy cream
2 tablespoons sugar
1 teaspoon fresh peppermint oil
1 tablespoon crème de menthe (optional)

Place the chocolate in a large bowl and set aside. Pour the milk, cream, and sugar into a heavy 1-quart saucepan and bring to a boil, whisking occasionally. Remove from the heat, pour over the chocolate, and let sit for 30 seconds. Whisk until smooth.

Add the peppermint oil and crème de menthe if desired and whisk until combined. Keep warm before serving. This sauce can be refrigerated for up to 1 week and thickens when chilled. To warm, heat the sauce in a 1-quart saucepan over low heat until liquid.

chocolate fantasy tower cake

YIELD: 10 TO 12 SERVINGS

This cake is an impressive crowd pleaser—especially when decorated with chocolate marble (page 162). It's called a tower because of its many layers and its appearance when a single square slice sits on a plate. This cake is not hard to make, but it has many components that can be made in stages ahead of time. The spiked peaks of meringue on top catch your eye and make you say "wow!," while a crunchy layer of meringue adds a wonderful textural and flavor contrast to the tang of the ganache.

Ganache:

8 ounces dark bittersweet chocolate (61% cacao), chopped finely

2 cups heavy cream

3 tablespoons sugar

¼ cup Greek yogurt or sour cream

Meringue:

Unsalted butter, softened, for greasing

4 large egg whites, at room temperature (about ½ cup)

Pinch salt

1 cup sugar

2 tablespoons blanched slivered almonds (optional)

About 3 ounces bittersweet chocolate, chopped fine

Cake:

⅔ cup cake flour

⅓ cup good-quality Dutch-process cocoa powder

4 large eggs, separated

¾ cup sugar

Pinch salt

Syrup:

¼ cup sugar
⅓ cup water

Glaze:

½ cup heavy cream
¾ cup water
¼ cup good-quality Dutch-process cocoa powder
½ cup sugar
7 ounces bittersweet chocolate, chopped fine

Prepare the ganache:

Place the chocolate in a medium bowl. In a heavy 1-quart saucepan, bring the cream and sugar to a boil. Pour over the chocolate and gently whisk until smooth and well combined. Add the yogurt or sour cream and whisk until smooth. Cover with plastic wrap and chill for 6 hours or overnight.

Prepare the meringue:

Place an oven rack in the middle position and preheat the oven to 225° F. Line a 12 x 17-inch sheet pan with parchment paper. Draw four 10 x 3½-inch rectangles on paper, invert the paper onto the sheet pan, then grease lightly with butter.

Pour the egg whites into a standing mixer fitted with a whisk attachment and whip on moderate speed. Add the salt when the egg whites begin to foam. Mix until soft peaks begin to form, about 3 minutes. Add ½ cup sugar gradually while mixing, until the mixture doubles in volume. Continue to mix until the mixture is shiny and glossy and stiff peaks form, about 5 minutes. Fold in the remaining sugar with a rubber spatula and transfer to a pastry bag fitted with a ¼-inch round tip.

Pipe the meringue into a tight zigzag pattern (about ¼ inch thick) on parchment paper to fill in the rectangles completely, about ⅓ inch thick. Decorate the top of one rectangle by piping sharp peaks as tightly as possible (like stalagmites). This will be your cake top, so be creative. Sprinkle almonds on the peaks if desired.

Bake until the meringue is crisp and dry, about 2 hours. Turn off the oven and leave the oven door slightly ajar, and leave overnight, or until the meringue is crisp. (The meringue will be slightly beige, and the top will take longer to dry.)

Melt the chocolate in a medium bowl over a pan of barely simmering water. (The bottom of the bowl should not touch the water.) Carefully brush the meringue on both sides with a light coating of chocolate to seal. For the decorative top, carefully invert and brush only the bottom side. (This will keep the meringue crisp in the cake layer.) Allow the chocolate to set at room temperature. (If the chocolate will not set, chill briefly just until it does.)

Note that it's best to make the meringue on a dry day, since humidity makes it soft and sticky. You can make the meringue ahead of time and keep it in an airtight container or wrapped gently, but securely, in plastic wrap.

Prepare the cake:

Place the oven rack in the middle position and preheat the oven to 350° F.

Line a 12 x 17-inch baking sheet pan with parchment paper.

Sift together the cake flour and cocoa powder two times.

In a standing mixer fitted with the whip attachment, mix the egg yolks with half the sugar on high speed until pale and fluffy, about 5 minutes; transfer to a bowl.

Whip the egg whites on moderate speed for 1 minute and add the salt. Continue to mix until the whites begin to form soft peaks, and gradually add the remaining sugar. Continue to mix until the mixture is shiny and forms stiff peaks, about 2 more minutes.

Using a rubber spatula, fold in the reserved egg-yolk mixture until just combined, then fold in the flour mixture until combined. Immediately pour the mixture into the prepared sheet pan, smoothing the top as necessary with an offset spatula. Tap lightly to release any air bubbles, and bake on the middle rack until the center springs back when lightly pressed or a toothpick inserted comes out clean, about 10 to 15 minutes. Cool on a wire rack.

Prepare the syrup:

Stir together the sugar and water in a heavy 1-quart saucepan over high heat until boiling. Remove from the heat. Use the syrup while warm.

Prepare the glaze:

Whisk together all of the glaze ingredients, except for the chocolate, in a heavy 2-quart saucepan until combined. Add the chocolate and stir constantly over moderately high heat until the chocolate has melted and the mixture just comes to a boil. Remove from the heat immediately and pour through a mesh strainer. Cool to room temperature.

To assemble the cake:

Once you have all of your components, it's time to "build the tower."

Lay a sheet of parchment paper on a large cutting board or work surface. Carefully invert the cake and gently peel off the parchment paper.

Brush the cake evenly, using all of the syrup. (It is easier to do when the syrup is warm.)

Transfer the chilled ganache to a standing mixer fitted with a whip attachment and mix on moderate speed until it forms stiff peaks, about 1 minute. (Be careful not to overmix or it can curdle.)

Using an offset spatula, spread the whipped ganache evenly on top of the cake. (If it is a warm day, chill the cake for 30 minutes before frosting.) Divide the cake into quarters along the long side of the cake (about 4 inches long) using a large heavy knife. Gently press one layer of meringue in the center of one cake quarter. Repeat with the remaining two layers and reserve the decorative top. One layer should remain without meringue. Freeze for 30 minutes, then carefully remove each layer of cake from parchment (use an offset spatula) and stack evenly, topping with the layer that has no meringue. Smooth the top with a warmed spatula if necessary, and freeze for 30 minutes.

Place the cake on a wire rack over a sheet pan. Pour the glaze over the cake, smoothing with a warmed spatula to even out the sides. When a smooth shape is achieved, you may pour any additional glaze on top. Keep refrigerated until serving. Place the top layer of spiked meringue decoration on just before serving. You may also decorate the sides of this cake with large pieces of chocolate marble (page 162) pressed against the sides.

To serve:

Cut the cake into 2-inch slices with a serrated knife dipped in hot water and wiped dry. Cut each slice in half again, to make 1-inch-thick slices or 2-inch square servings, and serve each guest his or her very own fantasy chocolate tower.

HOW TO DECORATE: TEMPER, MARBLE, DOODLE, CURL, AND COCOA TRANSFER

Temper

Decorations turn the simplest cake or dessert into something decadent and very special. Knowing a few simple tricks will last you a lifetime, but mastering the art of tempering chocolate can take time to learn. Tempering chocolate is done for recipes involving candy making or for decorations. Simply put, you are melting chocolate slowly, bringing the temperature up and then down and then holding it level while you work. This allows the crystals within the chocolate to balance and also allows proper hardening, which creates maximum shine and texture. It is simple to do in theory but can sometimes be frustrating in practice. Patience, practice, and a thermometer will yield stunning results. Once you know how to temper, the possibilities are endless. The techniques below are not a recipe per se; instead, they are guidelines for how to create wonderful garnishes and decorations.

You will need 1 pound of chocolate (any good couverture, not chips), chopped fine; six acetate sheets (from a florist or craft store); and two to three sheet pans measuring 12 x 17 inches or larger.

Have a large pot filled one-third full of barely simmering water (do not boil). Keep the heat on low. You must have very clean, dry utensils at all times—especially heatproof bowls and spatulas. Have a clean, large work surface and ample space in the refrigerator.

Place a heatproof bowl on top of the pot of simmering water. Be sure it is large enough to cover the surface of the pot without touching the water. Fill the bowl with three-quarters of the chocolate and slowly begin to melt.

Stir occasionally and keep an instant-read thermometer inserted. When the chocolate reaches 115° to 120° F, remove it from the heat and add the remaining quarter of the chocolate. Stir gently and constantly, allowing the added chocolate to melt slowly.

Let the temperature of the chocolate descend to a minimum temperature of 81° F and return the bowl to simmering water. (The chocolate may have lumps.) Stir gently and slowly, scraping down the sides, and allow the temperature to rise to between 86° and 91° F. If the chocolate becomes too hot, you can float the bowl in a larger bowl of cool but not cold water to help lower the temperature. Remove the chocolate, hold it at the proper temperature (see below) while you work, and stir occasionally. The chocolate may cool down and begin to solidify, at which point you should warm the bowl slightly over simmering water, taking care not to overheat it. As a test, you can dip the tip of a knife into melted chocolate. If the chocolate is properly tempered, it will harden in a minute.

With practice, you can temper chocolate without the use of a thermometer by touching it to your lip and comparing it to your body temperature, but using an accurate thermometer is foolproof.

The following are holding temperatures for different types of chocolate:

White and milk: 81° to 87° F

Semisweet (60% to 64%) and bittersweet (65% and up): 86° to 91° F

Note that there are many different ways to temper chocolate. You may choose the method you like best, but the bowl method is one of the easiest for home tempering. If you choose, you may cool a portion of the chocolate on a marble slab or vary temperatures in the microwave. Because most of us have a bowl and pot, the only other necessary piece of equipment is a good thermometer that can read low temperatures. (Marble slabs are heavy and large, and microwave ovens not only vary greatly in strength but also present difficulties in getting accurate temperature readings as you heat.)

Like methods for tempering, there are just as many varieties of chocolate. Aside from the ingredient content and percentages of cocoa butter, brands will also vary in texture from thin to thick. Choose one brand of chocolate to begin with and acclimate yourself to its nuances before going on to others.

This method is for chocolate that has been purchased ideally tempered. At times, drastic ranges in temperature will affect chocolate, causing gray-white chalky streaks to appear on its surface. This is called "blooming," and it's the result of cocoa butter forming crystals on the chocolate. Tempering the chocolate stabilizes these crystals. If you have badly bloomed or crystallized chocolate, melt as directed. If you have stubborn lumps that remain and refuse to go away, you can insert a clean, dry hand blender into the melted chocolate and pulse until the chocolate is smooth (be careful or you'll make a mess). As long as you exercise caution, this is a wonderful way to smooth chocolate quickly.

Marble

This is one of those decorations that inevitably garner applause. Edible marble—thick or thin—works as a wonderful border for cakes or as a garnish on a plated dessert. These sheets keep indefinitely, stored in a cool, dry place. Store flat on baking sheets wrapped tightly in plastic wrap.

You will need two different colors of chocolate, tempered, and two sheets (or more) of acetate (available at craft stores) or parchment paper.

Lay a sheet of acetate (shiny) or parchment paper (matte) on a flat work surface and using a rubber spatula, drizzle one type of chocolate evenly and generously, leaving a 3-inch border from the edge. Repeat with the remaining type of chocolate and cover directly with another sheet of acetate or parchment. Lightly roll with a rolling pin until desired thickness (or thinness) is achieved. Transfer to a flat baking sheet to harden. Repeat to make as many sheets as you wish. Break up pieces of chocolate marble to decorate the sides of any cake, or warm a cookie cutter and gently "punch" out shapes in the chocolate (be sure the chocolate is thick enough). Allow the chocolate to set and then remove.

Doodle

Writing in chocolate is a skill that takes getting used to. Once you get the hang of holding a cornet, you'll become more adept at drawing lines and eventually writing.

You will need tempered chocolate and a few sheets of parchment paper.

Have your chocolate ready and tempered as well as the surface you'd like to decorate. You can write directly onto a cake or simply on parchment paper for later use.

A cornet is a cone made of parchment paper, used to make a paper "pastry bag". The advantage to using a cornet as opposed to a standard pastry bag is that a very fine tip can be made easily with a snip of sharp scissors.

Cut a rectangle from your parchment paper. The size can vary, but use a minimum of 6 x 8 inches to begin with. Fold the paper diagonally, forming two right (or isosceles) triangles. Make a very sharp crease and cut clean through the paper.

Hold the triangle by the top point with the long side parallel to the floor. Bring the short side up, curling it into the top point to form a cone. Repeat with the other side to finish the cone and slide the paper with your fingers to adjust for a sharp tip. (Don't worry if the tops don't match; the point is the most important part.) Fold the top point inward, tucking it in. Hold the cornet or cone in your hand and carefully fill it with tempered chocolate about one-third full. Fold each top corner in and scroll down (like toothpaste) so the cornet is taut.

Snip the point with very sharp scissors. Remember that if the opening is too small, you can always cut a larger one.

Hold the cornet in your hand and squeeze gently to force chocolate out. Acclimate yourself to the flow of the chocolate (fast or slow) and move your hand in sync. As you squeeze, more chocolate will flow. When the cornet begins to empty, it is necessary to scroll the top (again, like toothpaste).

Practice first with little squiggles or designs. You may also use a pencil or pen to trace your desired design on one side of a piece of parchment paper and invert the paper, then pipe on the opposite side. Allow chocolate to harden and carefully lift off.

Curl

Chocolate curls are one of the easiest things to make! You will need one thick, large piece of chocolate, a vegetable peeler, and a melon ball scoop. When you want to make chocolate shavings, peel from a cold piece of chocolate. The results are chocolate bits that break up easily.

Curls require a bit of body warmth. Hold the chocolate in your hands to warm it slightly, but not until it is melting (just above body temperature). Run your peeler along a flat side of the chocolate and continue to warm after a few scrapes, then "peel" off a curl.

Another option is to scrape against a warmed piece of chocolate with a melon ball scoop, which will give you rounder-shaped curls.

This technique is easy but may take time to get used to. The first few curls or shavings may not be as beautiful as the last until you get the hang of it. Remember, you can always eat your mistakes!

Cocoa Transfer

Cocoa transfers are fun and draw "oohs and ahhs" whenever you present them. The simplest way to create them is to buy ready-made sheets from specialty cake-decoration shops such as NY Cake and Bake in Manhattan ([800] 942-2539) or online at www.sugarcraft.com; www.beryls.com; or www.kerekesequip.com. These acetate sheets have screened cocoa-butter designs that adhere to melted tempered chocolate. The designs vary from stripes and dots to images and even customized designs. The acetate sheets can be cut to any size or shape.

To make cut-out shapes or simple sheets of chocolate with a screened design on one side, simply pour tempered chocolate on top of the acetate sheet, spread evenly using a palette knife, and allow to harden. If you wish to have cut-out shapes, start to punch out shapes when the chocolate begins to firm. (It begins to take on a matte look and is still soft when touched.) The design will lift off the chocolate and appear on the shiny surface when the acetate is peeled back.

You can cut the transfer sheets into various shapes and create curls by draping sheets over objects such as a rolling pin and allowing the chocolate to harden. Gently peel back the acetate to release the chocolate.

Truffles can be dipped in tempered chocolate and dropped onto transfer sheets to give a unique design. Simply drop them onto the sheets after dipping them in chocolate and let them harden. Remove when the chocolate is set. This technique does not work for chocolates that have been dipped in anything other than tempered chocolate—for example cocoa powder or confectioners' sugar.

To make your own transfer designs, melt cocoa butter and mix it with small amounts of oil-soluble food coloring. Mix small amounts of the desired colors and paint your designs onto acetate. Let dry and proceed as directed above with tempered chocolate.

chocolate body scrub

YIELD: ONE BODY TREATMENT

Get yourself clean with this quick and easy body scrub. It's a great, all-natural exfoliant for the chocolate obsessed.

½ cup turbinado sugar
⅓ cup cocoa
2 tablespoons olive oil

Mix ingredients together thoroughly in a glass or plastic bowl. Apply the mixture to moistened skin and scrub. Rinse thoroughly.

It's that easy!

mudslide cookies

By Chef Jacques Torres of Jacques Torres Chocolate

YIELD: 20 LARGE COOKIES

Jacques and his highly skilled crew pump out the sweet stuff at the Jacques Torres Chocolate factory near the Brooklyn waterfront. Chocolate lovers are invited to be spectators at this fantasy-land where staff members in white aprons can be seen ferrying chocolate creations from station to station in a dizzying but precise dance. From cookies to hot chocolate, this cacao master knows how to keep the crowds satisfied.

Jacques is a fantastic person and we were thrilled that he offered his infamous Mudslide Cookies recipe for this book. Crisp on the outside, gooey on the inside—bake them and you'll see why they call him Mr. Chocolate.

6 ounces unsweetened chocolate
16 ounces bittersweet chocolate
⅜ cup unsalted butter, at room temperature
2 cups sugar
5 eggs
½ cup unbleached, all-purpose flour
2¾ teaspoons baking powder
1¼ teaspoons salt
Additional 16 ounces bittersweet chocolate chunks
1¼ cups walnuts, chopped (optional)

Preheat oven to 400°F. Line baking sheets with parchment paper. Melt the first two chocolates together. Set aside to cool.

Cream the butter and sugar with an electric mixer until light and fluffy. Add the eggs, one at a time, blending until mixed. Sift the flour, baking powder, and salt together, and then add to the butter mixture. Mix in the melted chocolate until combined.

Stir in the bittersweet chocolate chunks and nuts. Pour the mixture out onto a lined baking sheet. Place in the refrigerator for 5 to 10 minutes. It should be slightly, but not completely hardened.

Lay a piece of parchment paper on your work surface and reverse the chocolate onto it. Using a knife, divide the mixture into 20 squares. With your hands, roll each of the squares into a ball and place on one or two parchment-lined baking sheets, leaving room to allow them to spread.

Bake the cookies for 15 to 25 minutes or until they are crusty on the outside. Place on cooling racks and allow to cool at least 20 minutes before eating.

take a short cut.
delta.com/
DUTY

the quickest route to knowing everything chocolate

The story of chocolate is epic.

It is a drama overflowing with greed, royalty, bizarre myths, half-truths, and spontaneous inventions. Even if you consider yourself only a minor enthusiast, we highly recommend you delve deeper into the historical and factual worlds of chocolate. They are highly colorful.

At this time, we will not overburden you with the entire scope of all things chocolate. There will be no quiz and no final grade. This is our version of a *CliffsNotes* for chocolate. We hope you enjoy.

A VERY BRIEF HISTORY

The path of chocolate's history is intricate, winding, twisted, and very, very long, but here we offer you the speedy version. If you crave a more detailed account, check the sources section at the end of the book for several excellent books on chocolate's history.

Chocolate dates back to 200 A.D. when the Mayan people of Central and South America harvested cocoa beans from the cacao plant and ground them into a bitter, spicy drink. The drink was used in ceremonies as a celebratory beverage and as an offering to the gods.

The Aztecs eventually took to consuming chocolate around 1300 as their empire grew to include Mayan lands. It was during this time that cocoa beans became a form of money. Since the Aztecs could not grow cacao themselves, they traded other goods with the Mayans for cacao and demanded it as tribute to the emperor. Montezuma, the famous Aztec emperor who ruled from 1502 to 1520, was said to have consumed nearly fifty cups of chocolate a day. He believed it improved his performance when bedding his countless women. It's been rumored that his court ingested nearly 2,000 cups daily.

It was not until the 1520s that chocolate made its way to Europe—to Spain, in particular. The Spanish kept chocolate a secret from the rest of the continent for nearly one hundred years, making it just as the Aztecs and Mayans did, in liquid form, but adding sugar for sweetness. As the rest of Europe caught on to the chocolate sensation, it remained in liquid form and was often served as a treat for the royals and wealthy until the industrial revolution made chocolate production easier and swifter. Chocolate was hugely popular in the royal court of Louis XIV in the seventeenth century, but commoners didn't have access to the delicacy. Chocolate was available only from the South American colonies of Spain, and it was considered a drink of luxury. Yes, until the rise of the machine, our classic Hershey Bar didn't exist, and even plain old hot chocolate was elitist. So as much as we deplore the ozone-depleting, smog-producing monsters of steel, we have to love them for bringing chocolate to the masses.

Because of the difficulty of importing cacao from the Spanish-controlled regions of South America, European countries that caught the chocolate-loving bug enthusiastically founded cocoa-bean plantations in their colonies near the equator, where the environment is conducive to growing cacao trees. The English planted trees in Sri Lanka, the French in the West Indies, and the Dutch began growing cacao in Venezuela, Sumatra, and Java.

Although chocolate has been consumed for nearly 2,000 years, the solid chocolate bar wasn't invented until 1847. This seemingly minor invention changed the way the entire world viewed and consumed chocolate, inspiring not only variations of solid chocolate bars but chocolate truffles, cakes, cookies, and more. Hard to imagine, but chocolate Easter bunnies and Valentine's Day truffles didn't exist two centuries ago. The first edible Easter bunnies were made in Germany during the early 1800s and were made of pastry and sugar until chocolate became the norm. The heart-shaped candy box was created by Richard Cadbury (of Cadbury chocolates) in 1861. Once the solid chocolate bar made its rounds across the globe, various entrepreneurs and candy makers began experimenting. Milton Hershey first became intrigued with chocolate machinery at the Chicago International Exposition in 1893. He brought it back to Pennsylvania, where he began covering caramels in chocolate, and in 1894 the Hershey Chocolate Company was born. Thank you, Milton.

That stalwart homemade treat, the chocolate brownie, became available to all—all who shopped at Sears & Roebuck, that is—when the Sears & Roebuck catalogue printed a brownie recipe in 1897. Filled chocolates were first produced in Switzerland in 1913, and from then on, the world's chocolate makers refined and explored the ways of making bigger, better, and sweeter chocolate treats for the masses. It wasn't until the recent computer revolution that the ways chocolates were made changed. With the introduction of computers came the technology to create computerized enrobing machines, one-shot machines, and more. Speeding up the once time-consuming process of making chocolate truffles by hand, these machines can produce thousands of bonbons, truffles, and chocolate bars each day. And the innovations keep on coming. . . .

As international trade and globalization have become the normal way of life, chocolate in the twenty-first century is an ever-growing industry. There are varietal chocolates, artisanal chocolates, handmade truffles, molded chocolates, chocolate for baking, and chocolate for eating . . . yes, eating.

when they were created: a timeline of some of our favorite chocolates

1875 Daniel Peter and Henri Nestlé use condensed milk in chocolate, creating "milk chocolate"
1896 Tootsie Roll (Leo Hirschfield)
1900 Hershey Milk Chocolate Bar (Milton Hershey)
1904 Dairy Milk Bar (Cadbury)
1907 Hershey s Kisses (Milton Hershey)
1908 Toblerone Bar (Theodore Tobler)
1912 Whitman's Sampler (Whitman Company)
1912 Chocolate-covered pralines (Jean Neuhaus Jr., Neuhaus)
1914 Heath Bar (L. S. Heath & Sons)
1921 Mounds Bar (Peter Paul Halijian of Peter Paul Mounds)
1922 Reese's Peanut Butter Cups (H. B. Reese)
1923 Milky Way (Frank Mars of Mars Company)
1926 Godiva Molded Chocolates (Godiva Chocolate Company)
1930 Snickers (Mars Company)
1941 M&M's (Forrest Mars and Bruce Murrie [former President of Hershey] M&M Ltd.)
1949 Junior Mints (James Welch)
1978 Reese's Pieces (Hershey Foods Corporation)

CACAO & YOU

Tidbits, Notes, and Fun Facts About Our Favorite Food

■ Cacao is where chocolate comes from. It is the real deal. Cacao is also referred to as *cocoa solids* but is not cocoa as we know it.

■ The cacao tree can only grow and survive 20 degrees above or below the equator. The tree itself is fairly attractive, and in 1822, it was planted on Principe Island off Guinea, West Africa, as an ornamental plant. (Other uses quickly came to the forefront, and now African nations such as Ghana and the Ivory Coast produce millions of pounds of cocoa beans for export.)

■ The cacao tree prospers in rainforest conditions, producing the cacao pod, a big, striated melon-shaped thing that falls from its branches to the damp ground. Inside the foot-long pod are about twenty to forty cacao seeds, or cocoa beans. They ripen while the pod literally rots on the rainforest floor. It is the seeds that produce the chocolate we eat. They are fermented, dried, and ground to a paste that is eventually divided into two parts: cacao (chocolate) and cocoa butter. To create that sumptuous chocolate bar, you need both the cacao and the cocoa butter, along with sugar and milk solids. The cacao alone won't taste very good.

■ Chocolate is the number-one food craved by women across North America, and it's second to pizza among men. Currently, North Americans spend $8.9 billion per year on chocolate and consume nearly twelve pounds per person each year. And this is only the latest of statistics. Chocolate is one of the fastest-growing industries in the United States today. We are a nation, if not a world, of chocoholics.

■ Oddly enough, with all of the technological advances and new machinery, chocolate is grown, harvested, dried, and exported virtually the same way it was during the times of Aztec and Mayan rule. And though we think of chocolate as coming from Belgium, France, Switzerland, and the United States, it isn't actually from any of these countries. Chocolate is grown in countries such as Brazil, Venezuela, Colombia, Madagascar, and the Ivory Coast. Belgium, France, America, and other countries then import the cocoa beans and process them into the edible chocolate we so desperately desire.

■ The great debate over which country produces the best chocolate depends entirely on your personal taste. Chocolate varies widely from country to country and brand to brand. Try them all and find out what you like best. They all taste different.

■ White chocolate is a misnomer and contains no actual cacao. White chocolate is made from cocoa butter, milk solids, and sugar—not exactly the food groups recommended by the Surgeon General.

■ Chocolate can now be found as an ingredient in body-cleansing and moisturizing products and various prescription drugs. (Of course, cocoa butter has long been used in body moisturizers.) Along with its growing consumer popularity, chocolate is also the subject of more and more scientific research in hopes of finding new ways it can be used medically.

Buying, Storing, and Melting Chocolate

■ Always read the label. The fewer ingredients the better.

■ Store your chocolate (for baking or eating) in a cool, dry place. Avoid storing it in the fridge, since the moisture will create blooming (a harmless but ugly white film on the surface of the chocolate), and your chocolate may begin to taste like last night's Chinese takeout, since it readily absorbs other smells.

■ Chocolate starts to melt at 86° F. Don't leave your chocolate near a radiator, under your pillow, or on the stove.

■ Chocolate burns at 230° F. When melting chocolate for a recipe or fondue, it is best to do it slowly and not leave it unattended.

■ To melt chocolate on a stovetop, place evenly chopped pieces of chocolate in a heatproof bowl on top of a saucepan of steaming (but not boiling) water. The water level must be below the bottom of the bowl. Slowly and gently stir until the chocolate melts, then remove the pan from the heat immediately.

■ To melt chocolate in the microwave oven, place evenly chopped pieces of chocolate in a microwave-safe bowl and heat for 1 minute on low. When the minute is up, microwave in 15 second intervals until fully melted.

■ You may freeze chocolates (truffles, bonbons, bars for eating) if necessary. To do this properly, wrap the chocolate tightly in plastic wrap, place it in a paper bag, and put it in the freezer. When you are ready to eat it, remove it from the freezer and put it in the fridge for twelve hours (leave the wrap and bag on to prevent odor absorption or blooming). Remove from the fridge after twelve hours and leave, fully wrapped, on your counter for another twelve hours. Then remove the wrap and eat.

CHOCOLATE IS NOT GOING TO KILL YOU

Enough already! If you are going to eat chocolate you are going to consume calories, fat, and carbohydrates. Period. Stop worrying about it. There are a lot worse things in this world that you could put in your body. Eat chocolate. Enjoy chocolate. Hey, some of it is even good for you.

Chocolate CAN be Healthy

First and foremost, it is important you know that the higher the cacao content, meaning the actual chocolate itself, the healthier the chocolate. Chocolate has fallen victim to such ingredients as sugar, corn syrup, hydrogenated oils, fake chocolate, artificial preservatives, colors, and fillers. To get the best of the benefits along with the best taste, look for chocolate that is free of preservatives, has chocolate listed at the top of

• long lasting protection
.75fl oz./22ml
Purpose
Topical anesthetic
300ml
KIMAX
USA
NO. 14030

the ingredients list, and is made from ingredients you can pronounce (our biggest rule). All chocolate will have some sugar in it but does not need corn syrup or other fillers. The simpler the ingredients list, the purer your chocolate will be.

Get Happy

Chocolate does contain a certain amount of phenylethylamine, a known mild mood enhancer similar to the chemical our brain produces when we are happy. Feeling down? Down some chocolate!

Clean Your Teeth

Believe it or not, some research claims that dark chocolate prevents tooth decay! Not milk, not dark with caramel. Just plain dark. Although chocolate doesn't cause cavities, the added sugar does. Afraid of your dentist? Lay off the sweeter, lighter chocolates and indulge in deep darks.

A Spinach Substitute?

Chocolate contains stearic acid, a fat that does not raise bad cholesterol levels. As if that's not good enough news for high-cholesterol sufferers, cocoa butter, used in processing chocolate, contains the monounsaturated fat oleic acid, known to raise good cholesterol levels. Put down those fries and grab yourself a chocolate bar!

A Good Complexion

For those of us with sensitive, acne-prone skin, it may be a relief to find out that chocolate itself does not cause acne. Some believe it is the sugars and fillers that promote acne. We don t know this for sure so as we ve stated before, Chocolate Bar is an advocate of dark chocolate, which contains significantly less sugar than milk chocolate. And as always, we like to eat chocolate free of artificial colorings or preservatives.

Not the Buzz You Were Hoping For

Many pregnant women avoiding caffeine think they need to avoid chocolate. In reality, the average chocolate bar contains 6mg of caffeine, significantly less than the 100 to 150 mg found in one cup of coffee. As a matter of fact, a chocolate bar contains about as much caffeine as a cup of decaf.

Your Daily Intake of Vitamins and Minerals

The average 2.5-ounce bar of dark chocolate contains 3 grams of protein, 15 percent of the Daily Value of riboflavin, 9 percent of the Daily Value for calcium, and 7 percent of the Daily Value for iron.

ch
48

the obligatory stuff

KITCHEN EQUIPMENT

Every kitchen deserves to be equipped to impress. But realistically, the essentials are all that's needed. High-quality basics can go a long way in aiding your creative culinary efforts while minimizing the headaches. Investing in quality now will save you money, time, and frustration in the future. Trust us; we've tried the alternatives already! Here is a list of items we cherish and live by.

Measuring Tools

Good sets of stainless-steel measuring spoons and dry-measure cups are essential for exact measurements. (Remember that plastic sets can warp or melt.) Measuring-spoon sets can range from ⅛ teaspoon to 1 tablespoon, and dry-measure cups typically range from ¼ cup to 1 cup. Fill to the rim and level off with a straight edge for the most accurate measurement. Well-marked, clear glass measuring cups are necessary to measure liquid ingredients. These measures range in size from 1 to 4 cups. Look for cups that are microwavable and ovenproof.

Built-in oven thermometers can sometimes be a little off, which can lead to soggy cakes or burned cookies. An auxiliary mercury oven thermometer is a good gauge of your oven's calibration. Place it in a heated oven for 15 to 20 minutes, note the temperature, and compensate accordingly.

An instant-read thermometer (we like the digital kind because they're more precise) can spot-check the temperature of fillings or fudge and is an essential tool for a lot of our recipes.

Mixing, Stirring, Scraping, and Straining Tools

A heavy-duty countertop mixer is designed to mix, aerate, and knead large quantities of batters and dough without you having to do all the grunt work. The best standing mixers come equipped with a large stationary bowl and attachments such as a whisk, dough hook, and paddle. Handheld electric mixers can be used with almost any bowl and are great for smaller mixing jobs.

A nested set of mixing bowls is essential to every kitchen. Stainless-steel bowls are great for multipurpose work. They're durable and work well over hot water when melting chocolate. Glass, ceramic, and plastic bowls work wonders when recipes call for heatproof bowls.

Wooden spoons are useful for stirring and mixing, especially when done over heat. We keep our spoons for sweet recipes separate from those for savory, which can retain the taste of onion, chilies, and garlic. Stainless-steel spoons are great for testing tempered chocolate.

Rubber spatulas help you scrape every last bit of batter and mix from a bowl. They also work when folding ingredients together. Look for blades that measure 1 x 2 inches and 3 x 5 inches. An offset palette knife, which is a thin, round-tipped metal spatula with a crooked handle, is vital for frosting cakes and for working with tempered chocolate.

A pastry blender is a handy tool for making pastry dough. Its U-shaped wires cut fat into flour. A pastry scraper is great for cutting dough and for scraping it from counters and cutting boards. While we use one with a flat, rigid metal plate, they also come in plastic.

Sifters, made with very fine wire mesh, are used to aerate flour and other dry ingredients for baking. Recipes will say whether or not you should sift before measuring. Mesh strainers are used to separate solids from liquids.

Stovetop and Bakeware

Whether you're melting chocolate or making marmalade, we recommend you use top-quality, heavy saucepans. Lightweight pans might be less expensive but they dent, wear out quickly, and often conduct heat unevenly. Your kitchen's not complete without a good, basic selection of saucepans, including 1-, 2-, and 3-quart sizes.

A double boiler, which is essentially two stacked saucepans, provides gentler heat for melting and warming foods. The boiling water in the lower saucepan provides the heat to the top saucepan. If you don't own a double boiler, you can improvise by placing a metal bowl over a pot of boiling water. Make sure the bowl does not touch the water.

The finish on your baking pans and sheets is an important factor to be aware of. Darker-colored pans rapidly absorb and convey heat to produce heavier, browner crusts, while tinned steel and aluminum finishes deflect some of the oven heat to produce golden crusts. As with your other kitchen equipment, the range for metal bakeware is broad. Heavier-gauge, reinforced pans and sheets might cost more, but they will last for years and help create better-looking baked goods.

Cookie sheets are flat and rimless (or have a rim on only one end). Heavy-duty cookie sheets are the only way to go. Thin ones buckle, and you can end up with unevenly baked cookies.

Cake pans range in size and depth, but we recommend owning at least two 9 x 2-inch round layer cake pans, one 9 x 9 x 2-inch pan, and one 13 x 9 x 2-inch pan.

Half-sheet pans, also known as jelly roll pans, vary in size, but we like 17 x 12-inch pans. They're great for sheet cakes and bar cookies.

While you can buy muffin pans for mini- or megamuffins and cupcakes, a standard muffin pan with twelve cups is an essential.

A 9- or 10-inch shallow tinned steel tart pan with a removable bottom and a set of mini (4-inch) nonstick tart molds are handy for baking our filled tart recipes.

Pie plates come in all sizes and materials. We prefer aluminum plates for filled pies because the crust won't overly brown before the inside is cooked. Black steel pie plates work wonderfully to bake and brown an unfilled crust quickly.

Most metal or glass loaf pans measure 9 x 5 x 3 inches. Remember, if you're baking in a glass pan, cakes may brown before they are thoroughly baked, so reduce the oven temperature by 25° F.

For the Fanatic

For those of us who spend more time in the kitchen than usual, here are some additional tools we are fond of but which are not necessary to create an efficient kitchen (unless called for in a recipe). Remember, you can always borrow from Mom, Sis, or that neighbor you've become acquainted with. Just remember to share your goodies when you're done!

- food processor
- gelatin molds
- hand blender
- pastry bag and tips
- pastry board
- pastry cloth
- pie weights
- propane torch
- ramekins
- rolling pin
- wire cooling racks

GLOSSARY

Alkalized Cocoa Powder—cocoa powder with a deeper color and more intense flavor than the regular variety. Alkalized cocoa powder allows you to use less cocoa while achieving the same taste. The alkalization process neutralizes acidic components in the cocoa, removing some of its astringency and contributing to a more well-rounded flavor profile.

Baking Chocolate—a type of chocolate used in baking; it is usually very bitter, as it contains no sugar.

Bitter Chocolate—any chocolate comprised of *cacao* and *cocoa butter* without the addition of sugar.

Bittersweet Chocolate—chocolate comprised of at least 60% *cacao* with minimal sugar added.

Bloom—a coating that develops on chocolates when the sugar separates from the *cacao* and *cocoa butter,* creating a dusty white appearance. Although blooming does not generally affect the taste of chocolate, it is not pretty to look at.

Cacao—a subtropical tree that produces *cacao* pods, the seeds of which are used in making chocolate.

Cacao Content—the amount of actual *cacao* present in chocolate.

Carob—a Mediterranean evergreen tree in the pea family used widely as a chocolate substitute in vegan desserts.

Chocolate Chips—small pieces of chocolate used in baking or making chocolate-chip cookies.

Chocolate Liquor—a product produced by grinding the cocoa bean center into a smooth, liquid state.

Chocolatier—a person who works with chocolate to make candies, truffles, bars, etc.

Cocoa—a powder made from *cacao* seeds after they have been fermented, roasted, shelled, ground, and freed of most of their fat.

Cocoa Beans—*cacao* seeds.

Cocoa Butter—the fat present in *cacao* seeds and used in the process of making chocolate.

Cocoa Powder—*cocoa*

Conching—the process by which machines stir chocolate to insure it's blended evenly. It's one of the last steps performed in manufacturing and can take anywhere from a few hours to a few days to complete.

Confectioner—one who makes confections.

Confectionery Coating—chocolate disks used for dipping fruit or candies in when melted. Confectionery coating dries much faster and shinier than real chocolate and is available in milk, dark, or white chocolate.

Couverture—the outer chocolate coating of a *truffle.*

Dark Chocolate—similar to *bittersweet chocolate,* containing no less than 50% cacao.

Enrobing—the process of applying chocolate *couverture* over a truffle *ganache.*

Fondant—a sweet, creamy sugar paste used in candies and icings.

Ganache—the inside of a *truffle*, made of chocolate and cream.

Lecithin—an emulsifier used in chocolate to reduce viscosity, or thickness.

Milk Chocolate—any chocolate comprised of less than 40% *cacao*. Milk, *cocoa butter,* and sugar make up the majority of this kind of chocolate.

Mocha—a blend of chocolate and espresso or other coffee.

Mole—a Mexican sauce, said to have been created in the seventeenth century in Puebla by a Dominican nun. The traditional recipe has more than thirty different ingredients.

Molinillo—a Spanish tool used to froth hot chocolate.

Nibs—the centers of *cacao* seeds.

Semisweet Chocolate—*bittersweet chocolate.*

Sweet Chocolate—chocolate sweetened with sugar.

Tempering—the process of turning melted chocolate into a solid mass of stable *cocoa butter* crystals with fine, even-grained texture through carefully heating and cooling the chocolate.

Theobroma—cacao plant.

Truffle—any type of chocolate treat that includes a *ganache* and *couverture*.

Unsweetened Chocolate—chocolate without the addition of sugar.

Viscosity—the resistance to flow in fluid or partial fluid.

White Chocolate—a misnomer; white chocolate is not chocolate at all. There is no *cacao* present in white chocolate, only *cocoa butter,* milk solids, and sugar.

Xocolatl—Aztec word for "bitter water," from which the word "chocolate" is derived. The Aztecs drank *xocolatl*, which was a mixture made from ground-up *cacao* tree seeds and spices.

Sugars

Confectioners' Sugar—a refined finely powdered sugar
Demerara Sugar—raw unprocessed sugar
Granulated Sugar—the standard, widely used form of pure white sugar
Sanding Sugar—sugar with a grain slightly coarser than that of granulated sugar. It comes in vivid colors and can be used either before or after baking
Turbinado Sugar—a raw sugar that is obtained or crystallized from the initial pressing of sugar cane

WHERE TO BUY

Chocolate

Abuelita Mexican Chocolate by Nestlé
www.mexgrocer.com

Barry Callebaut
www.barry-callebout.com

E. Guittard Chocolate
www.eguittard.com

Ibarra Mexican Chocolate
www.chocoibarra.com.mx

Valrhona Chocolate
www.valrhona.com

Cocoa Transfer Sheets

Beryls Cake Decorating and Pastry Supplies
www.beryls.com

Kerekes Bakery and Restaurant Equipment
www.kerekesequip.com

New York Cake and Bake
www.nycake.com

Sugar Craft Cake Decorating and Candy Making Products
www.sugarcraft.com

Liquor

Grand Marnier Cognac
www.grand-marnier.com

Hennessy VSOP
www.hennessy-cognac.com

Johnnie Walker Black Scotch
www.johnniewalker.com

Stoli Vanilla Vodka
www.stoli.com

Vermeer Dutch Chocolate Cream
www.vermeercream.com

Vanilla, Sugar, and Espresso

Charles H. Baldwin & Sons Vanilla Extract
www.baldwinextracts.com

Illy Caffè
www.illyusa.com

Nielsen Massey Vanilla Extract, Beans, and Paste
www.nielsenmassey.com

Sweet Celebrations Candy Making Supplies
www.sweetc.com

Kitchen Equipment

Bridge Kitchenware
www.bridgekitchenware.com

Broadway Panhandler
www.broadwaypanhandler.com

JB Prince
www.jbprince.com

KitchenAid
www.kitchenaid.com

Polder Home Tools
www.polder.com

Zabar's
www.zabars.com

Chocolate Body Products

Fresh
www.fresh.com

MAC Cosmetics
www.maccosmetics.com

Philosophy
www.philosophy.com

Sephora
www.sephora.com

ADDITIONAL SOURCES OF INFO

Books

Bloom, Carol. *All About Chocolate.* New York: Hungry Minds, 1998.

Boyle, Tish. *Diner Desserts.* San Francisco: Chronicle Books, 2000.

Brenner, Joel Glenn. *Emperors of Chocolate: Inside the Secret World of Hershey and Mars.* New York: Broadway Books, 2000.

Coe, Sophie D. and Michael D. *The True History of Chocolate.* London: Thames & Hudson, 2000.

Kimmerle, Beth. *Candy: The Sweet History.* Portland, OR: Collectors Press, 2003.

Malgieri, Nick. *Chocolate: From Simple Cookies to Extravagant Showstoppers.* New York: HarperCollins, 1998.

Martínez, Zarela. *The Food and Life of Oaxaca.* New York: John Wiley & Sons, 1997.

Morton, Marcia and Frederic. *Chocolate: An Illustrated History.* New York: Random House, 1986.

Torres, Jacques. *Dessert Circus: Extraordinary Desserts You Can Make at Home.* New York: Morrow Cookbooks, 1998.

Websites

Barry Callebaut: www.barry-callebaut.com
Chicago's Field Museum: www.fmnh.org
Chocolate Manufacturers Association: www.candyusa.org
Hershey Foods Corporation: www.hershey.com
World Cocoa Foundation: chocolateandcocoa.org

INDEX